Isles of Scilly T Guide 2023

A Comprehensive Adventure Guide to Discover Nature, Island Adventures and Much More + 7-Day Itinerary

By Larry E. Miller

Copyright

All rights reserved. No part of this publication may be reproduced, distributed, or transmitted in any form or by any means, including photocopying, recording, or other electronic or mechanical methods, without the prior written permission of the publisher, except in the case of brief quotations embodied in critical reviews and certain other noncommercial uses permitted by copyright law.

Copyright © Larry E. Miller, 2023.

Introduction: My Journey to the Isles of Scilly

The ebb and flow of life's rhythms, sometimes call us to seek out the unusual and escape the mundane. As a seasoned traveler and ardent explorer, I found myself longing for such a respite—a journey that would take me to a place of tranquility, beauty, and discovery. Little did I realize that the Isles of Scilly would form the backdrop for this engrossing adventure, a story that would live on in my mind for the rest of my life.

It all started on a clear morning when I stepped into the beaches of St. Mary's, the biggest of the Isles. The ocean breeze welcomed me like an old friend, whispering stories of sailors and untold tales. In Hugh Town, the island's capital, history smoothly embraced the present as cobblestone streets led to stores embellished with handcrafted goods and treasures unique to the Isles.

Beyond the busy streets, though, I discovered the genuine soul of these enchanting isles. With each step down the coast, I found quiet coves with pristine sands and waters touched by blues I'd never seen before. I set out on trails that went through meadows strewn with vivid wildflowers, a surprise splash of color against the canvas of the Atlantic.

The lure of adventure took me to Tresco one morning, where the world-renowned Tresco Abbey Garden stood as a tribute to nature's tenacity. I found peace among the exotic blossoms and vivid foliage—an island of tranquility that appeared worlds away from the mainland's problems.

Time seemed to linger on St. Martin's, enabling me to relish each moment as if it were a valuable treasure. The island's attractions were revealed via sandy roads that wove through aromatic heathlands, leading to turquoise bays that glistened like gems. The simple act of drinking tea at a quaint café seemed ritualistic, each sip filled with the laid-back charm of the island.

However, it was the native tales that built a picture of these islands. Stories of perseverance and camaraderie emerged when I interacted with the islanders. They spoke of community events and the connection they had with the land and sea that surrounded them. Their kindness and friendliness created an unforgettable impression, transforming strangers into friends in an instant.

As the sun set below the horizon, throwing a golden glow on the waves, I understood that the Isles of Scilly were more than simply a stopover; they were a chapter in a vast voyage. The days flew by, but the memories I made during my vacation would live on in my heart forever.

I encourage you to stroll beside me on the cobblestone streets, breathe in the salty breeze, and immerse yourself in the beauty of these islands with this guidebook. Allow these pages to serve as your guide to discovering hidden gems, enjoying island life, and crafting your tale amongst the beauty of the Isles of Scilly.

Welcome to a destination where every moment is an opportunity to go on an adventure.

Table of Contents

Copyright... 2

Introduction: My Journey to the Isles of Scilly............... 3

Table of Contents... 6

Chapter 1: Introduction to the Isles of Scilly................ 11

    Welcome to the Isles of Scilly..................................... 11

    A Brief Historical Overview..14

    Unique Charms of the Islands.................................... 16

    Setting Your Expectations.. 19

Chapter 2: Planning Your Trip......................................23

    Climate and Best Times to Visit................................ 23

    Travel Documents and Visa Information....................26

Packing Essentials... 31

Getting to the Isles of Scilly....................................... 33

Navigating the Islands... 36

Chapter 3: Accommodation Guide............................ 40

Choosing Your Island Base..40

Luxury Resorts and Boutique Hotels.........................42

Charming Bed and Breakfasts................................... 46

Self-Catering Cottages and Rentals........................... 51

Chapter 4: Exploring the Natural Beauty...................... 53

Pristine Beaches and Coastal Marvels.......................53

Nature Reserves and Wildlife Habitats......................56

Guided Birdwatching Tours.......................................60

Gardens and Botanical Wonders................................62

Island Hiking Trails: Nature Walks and Scenic Views.. 65

Chapter 5: Island Adventures... 69

Water Sports and Aquatic Activities..........................69

Biking Trails and Cycling Routes..............................72

Historical Sites and Landmarks.................................. 74

Lighthouses and Maritime History............................ 78

Unique Experiences: From Boat Tours to Rock Climbing.. 80

Chapter 6: Embracing Island Culture............................ 84

Engaging with Islanders.. 84

Local Etiquette and Customs..................................... 86

Festivals and Events.. 89

Local Arts and Crafts Traditions................................ 93

Visiting Museums and Cultural Centers.................... 96

Chapter 7: Gastronomic Delights: Dining on the Isles 100

Island Flavors: A Culinary Introduction................. 100

Local Cuisine and Seafood Specialties.................... 103

Dining Establishments Overview............................ 106

Chapter 8: Relaxation and Wellness............................ 110

Spa and Wellness Retreats....................................... 110

Yoga and Meditation Escapes.................................. 113

Rejuvenating by the Sea.. 116

Local Holistic Practices.. 119

Chapter 9: Island Hopping in the Isles of Scilly.......... 123

　How to Island Hop.. 123

　Things to do on Each Island..................................... 126

　Island Hopping Tips... 129

Chapter 10: Shopping and Souvenirs........................... 133

　Retail Therapy on the Isles....................................... 133

　Unique Souvenirs to Bring Home............................. 136

　Markets and Shops to Explore.................................. 139

Chapter 11: 7-Day Itinerary.. 144

　Day 1: Arrival and Island Orientation...................... 144

　Days 2-3: Coastal Exploration and Water Adventures.. 147

　Days 4-5: Nature Immersion and Cultural Experiences 150

　Day 6: Wellness and Tranquility.............................. 153

　Day 7: Farewell and Reflections.............................. 157

Chapter 12: Practical Information................................. 161

Health and Safety Tips... 161

Useful Phrases and Local Language........................ 164

Currency, Banking, and Local Services.................... 167

Staying Connected: Internet and Communication... 171

Essential Contacts and Websites.............................. 174

Conclusion.. 178

Chapter 1: Introduction to the Isles of Scilly

Welcome to the Isles of Scilly

The Isles of Scilly appeared on the horizon like a collection of magnificent pearls embellishing the ocean's embrace as the ferry's bow slashed through the cerulean waters. Stepping upon these shores seemed like entering a world unspoiled by the rushed pace of contemporary life, a place where nature and history coexist in harmonic magnificence.

The Isles of Scilly are more than simply a vacation spot; they are a sensory haven. A soothing tranquility overwhelmed me the minute I stepped foot on St. Mary's, the largest of the islands. The salty air brought whispers of years gone by, while the craggy landscapes stood like silent storytellers, ready to share their tales with anyone who listened.

Hugh Town, on St. Mary's, offers a charming introduction to island life. Cobblestone streets lead to lovely cafes, boutiques with one-of-a-kind treasures, and a feeling of community as warm as the sun's embrace. The Garrison Walls, relics of a fortified past, remind us of the islands' historical importance as well as the tenacity of men who formerly traveled these roads.

But it's not only history that colors the Isles' canvas; it's also the wild beauty that demands exploration. Tresco, only a short boat journey away, is a different world—a subtropical oasis where the Tresco Abbey Garden is brimming with brilliant life. You may immerse yourself in a symphony of colors and fragrances here while surrounding beaches invite you to luxuriate in nature's embrace.

St. Martin's, with its unspoiled beaches and tranquil atmosphere, provides a peek into a gentler way of life. The rhythm of the island is determined by the tides, the whispering breezes, and the soothing lull of the waves. It's a location where you may walk along sandy shores and let the concerns of the world wash away with each step.

The adventurer and the dreamer are drawn to Bryher's rough beauty and creative energy. Hike its trails to experience spectacular vistas that will take your breath away. You'll sense a connection to the ancient forces that sculpted these islands as the sun slips below the horizon, filling the sky with brilliant colors.

Then there's St. Agnes, the smallest inhabited island in the world, where every turn is an intimate experience with nature's splendor. You'll come face to face with spectacular landscapes as you explore its paths, making you feel like you're standing on the edge of the planet.

Welcome to the Isles of Scilly, where time seems to stop, nature's beauty unfolds in its entire splendor, and the genuine kindness of the islanders makes you feel like family. Prepare to be captured by the tranquility, attraction, and magic that characterize this unique archipelago as you stroll through these pages.

A Brief Historical Overview

The Isles of Scilly, a collection of ancient gems situated amid the broad expanse of the Atlantic, hold the whispers of centuries past within their shores. These islands have seen a tapestry of history that dates back millennia, leaving remnants that still ring true today.

The Isles of Scilly were home to Neolithic cultures that left behind their legacy in the shape of cryptic monuments dating back to the mists of time. The Bant's Carn on St. Mary's is a tribute to their creativity, a community mausoleum that has stood the test of time. Each stone seems to protect the secrets of people who have trod these shores in the past.

Throughout history, the islands have seen the arrivals and departures of explorers, merchants, and attackers. Because of their strategic position, they were a critical crossroads in maritime history. The St. Mary's Garrison Walls, built during the English Civil War, serve as silent sentinels to a period when the islands played a critical part in defending the realm.

The maritime heritage runs through the blood of the Isles, and the Valhalla Collection on Tresco honors this legacy. The shipwreck museum displays rescued figureheads and artifacts from boats that met their demise along the rocky coastline. Each sculpture conveys a tale of maritime undertakings, reminding us of the islanders' tenacity in their relationship with the sea.

Art and literature have also sought refuge in these islands' embrace. Writers and painters have sought inspiration here, captivated by the natural beauty and tranquility. Sir Arthur Quiller-Couch sought refuge and inspiration among them, leaving an enduring imprint on the cultural fabric of the Isles.

Today, when you walk the Isles of Scilly, you are following in the footsteps of previous generations. The historic fortresses, ancient stones, and maritime relics are more than simply artifacts; they are chapters in a living history book. In this story, the islands themselves are people, their landscapes ringing with the tales of explorers, mariners, and visionaries.

Take a minute to listen on your way to the Isles, to hear the echoes of the past that linger in the air, and to appreciate the layers of history that have sculpted these lovely shores. As you take in the beauty and charm of the islands, keep in mind that you are becoming a part of their continuous tale, leaving imprints that will join the chorus of history.

Unique Charms of the Islands

The Isles of Scilly, an archipelago of unsurpassed beauty cradled in the embrace of the Atlantic, have a universe of distinct charms that beg to be discovered. The Isles provide a rich tapestry of experiences that appeal to every traveler's thirst for adventure and tranquility, with each island possessing its character and attraction.

St. Mary's: The Isles' Heartbeat

St. Mary's, the largest and most central island, welcomes guests with open arms and ageless charm. Hugh Town, the lively center, enchants with cobblestone streets, friendly cafes, and handmade stores showcasing the islands' artistry. Explore the historic Garrison Walls, which remain as stalwart sentinels from another age. St. Mary's is the archipelago's entry point, where both adventure and leisure await.

Tresco: A Subtropical Paradise

Tresco, a short boat trip away, brings you to a world where gardens blossom with astounding variety. The Tresco Abbey Garden, a paradise of rare and exotic flora, provides a tranquil retreat for reflection. The beaches on the island have virtually white sand that contrasts well with the bright blue waters. Tresco combines relaxation with the wonder of botanical discovery in a seamless way.

St. Martin's: Serenity on the Sands

St. Martin's, the picturesque island of tranquility, is a haven for beachgoers and those looking for quiet. Its pristine beaches are surrounded by blue waters that beckon you to take a refreshing swim or snorkel lazily. The tiny population of the island generates a feeling of community, where locals and tourists coexist in peaceful harmony. St. Martin's is a haven for individuals looking for simplicity and connection with nature.

Bryher: Rugged Beauty and Artistic Soul

Bryher's craggy landscapes and natural beauty serve as a blank canvas for outdoor adventure. Explore the island's rugged paths, soaking in panoramic vistas and discovering hidden jewels along the route. The majestic cliffs and windswept shores inspire creative spirits. The wild attraction of Bryher draws travelers to uncover its mysteries.

St. Agnes: Nature's Intimate Hideaway

St. Agnes, the smallest inhabited island, envelops every visitor with an impression of closeness and tranquility. As you walk its trails, you'll see breathtaking vistas and pristine natural beauty at every turn. St. Agnes offers the opportunity to embrace seclusion and engage with the natural elements that have created these islands for millennia.

The Isles of Scilly are a symphony of diverse charms, where the various personalities of the islands blend to create an unforgettable melody of experiences. Whether you want to immerse yourself in history, relax in a subtropical sanctuary, or wander free among harsh landscapes, the Isles offer a charm for everyone. May you find the enchantment that lies inside each island's embrace when you tread upon these shores.

Setting Your Expectations

As you prepare to go to the Isles of Scilly, it's critical to build an attitude of curiosity mixed with island tranquility. These enthralling isles are a refuge of natural beauty, rich culture, and a way of life that moves to its peaceful cadence.

Time on the Island

When you arrive at the Isles of Scilly, you'll discover that time moves a little differently. The frantic tempo of the mainland is replaced with a more relaxed pace. Accept this shift as an opportunity to escape the everyday grind, enabling you to stroll without hurry and thoroughly absorb the spirit of the island. Engage in leisurely chats with locals who are eager to share their stories.

Nature's Whimsy

The weather on the islands may be as volatile as the tides, which adds to their charm. Prepare for times when the sun and rain playfully dance, painting the sky with stunning colors. Dress in layers and bring a light raincoat to be prepared for anything Mother Nature chooses to display. Remember that changing weather patterns are nature's method of keeping landscapes lively and dynamic.

Disconnect to Reconnect

While the Isles of Scilly provide contemporary conveniences, they also promote separation from the digital world. Cell phone service may not be as ubiquitous as you're accustomed to, but that's on purpose. Consider it a subtle reminder to immerse oneself in the current moment. Put your electronics aside and allow the sound of the sea and the melodies of the island be your friends.

Embrace Island Indulgences

The Isles of Scilly provide a diverse range of activities that set them apart from other popular tourist locations. Expect no lavish amusement parks or busy business areas. Instead, experience the pleasures of outdoor adventure, meaningful connections with locals, and wonderful island food. Enjoy the simple pleasures that these shores have to offer.

Flexibility and Spontaneity

Allow for some spontaneity in your island vacation. Unplanned moments may provide the most treasured memories—a detour along a gorgeous route, an unexpected beach lunch, or a compelling talks with a local artist. The key to properly experiencing the Isles' surprise treasures is flexibility.

Allow your expectations to coincide with the island's intrinsic spirit—a combination of tranquility, genuineness, and an unwavering connection to nature. The Isles of Scilly invite you to slow down, reconnect with nature, and revel in the real delights of island existence.

Chapter 2: Planning Your Trip

Climate and Best Times to Visit

Ah, let's talk about one of the most vital aspects of planning your island adventure—the weather. The Isles of Scilly boast a maritime climate, which means that Mother Nature has a knack for keeping things interesting. Picture sunny days giving way to brief showers, and then back to sunshine—all in the blink of an eye. It's a climate that adds a touch of unpredictability, but believe me, it's all part of the Isles' charm.

Seasonal Symphony

Spring (March to May): Spring is a bit like a painter's palette, with flowers bursting into bloom and the landscape coming alive with vibrant hues. Temperatures hover around 50-60°F (10-15°C), making it a refreshing time to explore. Pack layers, including a light waterproof jacket, because those April showers are real, and they tend to surprise you with their timing.

Summer (June to August): The Isles shine their brightest. Average temperatures range from 60-70°F (15-20°C), and the sun graces the islands with its presence for longer stretches. Beach days, coastal hikes, and leisurely boat trips are on the agenda. Just remember to pack sunscreen and sunglasses to protect yourself from those sunny rays.

Autumn (September to November): The autumnal landscape takes center stage as the islands transition into a symphony of rich colors. Temperatures begin to cool down to the 50s°F (10-15°C), and this quieter season is perfect for those who relish a bit of solitude amidst nature's spectacle. A good rainproof jacket is your ally, as showers become more frequent.

Winter (December to February): Winter brings a sense of serenity to the Isles. Temperatures dip into the 40s°F (5-10°C), and while it might not be prime beach weather, the landscapes possess a certain wild beauty. It's an excellent time for birdwatching and embracing the islands' quietude. Remember to layer up, and don't forget your scarf and gloves to keep the chill at bay.

Timing is Key

Peak Season: The summer months of June to August draw the most visitors, thanks to the pleasant weather and a calendar bustling with events. Accommodations might fill up quicker during this time, so it's wise to book ahead. And let's not forget the world-famous Tresco Abbey Garden's Flower Show in May—an explosion of color you won't want to miss.

Shoulder Seasons: Spring and autumn offer a more intimate experience, with milder weather and fewer crowds. If you're after a balance between pleasant weather and a quieter atmosphere, these are your go-to months.

Winter Wanderings: While winter sees fewer visitors, it's a chance to experience the Isles in their most serene state. If you're seeking solitude, a deeper connection with the landscape, and a chance to truly unwind, this might be the season for you.

So, there you have it—a whirlwind tour of the Isles' weather and the best times to visit. Remember, the Isles of Scilly are a treasure trove of experiences no matter the season. Just pack with a hint of adaptability, embrace the island's ever-changing weather mood, and you're all set to embark on a truly unforgettable journey.

Travel Documents and Visa Information

Ahoy there, fellow traveler! Let's chat about the nitty-gritty essentials that'll get you to our beloved Isles of Scilly. Now, while you won't need an actual treasure map, you'll need a set of documents that'll ensure your journey is as smooth as the waves off our shores.

Passport Power
First things first—a valid passport is your golden ticket to the Isles. Make sure it's good for at least six months

beyond your planned departure date. That's the rule of thumb here, and it'll ensure you're all set for your island escapade.

Visa Voyage

Citizens of the following countries/territories do not need a visa to visit the Isles of Scilly for tourism purposes:

1. All EU countries
2. Andorra
3. Antigua and Barbuda
4. Argentina
5. Australia, Bahamas
6. Barbados
7. Belize
8. Botswana
9. Brazil
10. Brunei
11. Canada
12. Chile
13. Costa Rica

14. El Salvador
15. Grenada
16. Guatemala
17. Hong Kong
18. Israel
19. Japan
20. Kiribati
21. Macau
22. Malaysia
23. Maldives
24. Marshall Islands
25. Mauritius
26. Mexico
27. Monaco
28. Micronesia
29. Nauru
30. New Zealand
31. Nicaragua
32. Palau
33. Panama
34. Papua New Guinea
35. Paraguay

36. Saint Kitts and Nevis
37. Saint Lucia
38. Saint Vincent and the Grenadines
39. Samoa
40. San Marino
41. Seychelles
42. Singapore
43. Solomon Islands
44. South Korea
45. Tonga
46. Trinidad and Tobago
47. Tuvalu
48. United States of America
49. Uruguay
50. Vatican City.

Citizens of countries not listed above should check the official UK government website (www.gov.uk) or consult with their local consulate to know about how and what they need to apply for a tourist visa. It's always best to double-check the rules and regulations before you set sail.

If you require a visa to travel to the Isles of Scilly, it's advisable you apply two weeks prior to your intended trip to allow enough time for the processing.

Travel Insurance

While it's not a legal requirement to visit the Isles, having travel insurance is a smart move. It covers everything from lost luggage to unexpected mishaps. Plus, it's peace of mind knowing you're covered for life's little surprises.

Remember, the Isles of Scilly are a slice of paradise, and we're thrilled to welcome you here. Just make sure your travel documents are in shipshape order, and you'll be ready to soak in the beauty and adventure that await.

Packing Essentials

Ahoy, fellow traveler! If you're about to embark on a journey to the Isles of Scilly, let's have a little chat about packing. You see, our islands are a blend of adventure and relaxation, so you'll want to make sure you're equipped for all the wonderful surprises our shores have in store.

Island-Ready Attire

Let's start with the basics—what to wear. The key here is layers. Our maritime climate is a bit like a chameleon—ever-changing. So, pack lightweight shirts, comfy trousers or shorts, and a trusty sweater or hoodie for those breezy moments. And, of course, a good rainproof jacket is your knight in shining armor against those unexpected showers.

Don't forget swimwear—our pristine beaches and clear waters are a siren call for a refreshing dip. And speaking of beaches, a sun hat and sunglasses are your partners in crime against the sunny rays.

Footwear for Every Adventure

Ah, the island terrain—sometimes rugged, sometimes sandy, always breathtaking. Pack comfortable walking shoes for exploring our trails and beaches. Sandals or flip-flops are great for strolling by the shore, and trust me, your feet will thank you after a day of island adventures.

Tech and Gadgets

While we encourage a bit of digital detox, you'll still want to capture those picture-perfect moments. So, a trusty camera or smartphone is a must. And don't forget chargers—you wouldn't want your gadgets to run out of juice just when you're about to snap a stunning sunset, would you?

Creature Comforts

Now, let's talk about comfort. A reusable water bottle is a lifesaver, keeping you hydrated as you explore. And a backpack to carry your essentials is a lifesaver for your shoulders. Throw in some snacks for those impromptu picnics—you'll find plenty of picturesque spots that practically beg for a nibble.

Extras that Add Magic

Here's where you can add a touch of your own magic to your packing list. A good book to dive into during quiet moments, a journal to jot down your island musings, and perhaps a local guidebook for a deeper understanding of our beloved Isles.

And the Golden Rule: Pack Adaptability
Remember, the Isles of Scilly are a bit like a box of assorted chocolates—each day brings something new. So, pack with a dash of adaptability and a pinch of curiosity. Embrace the ever-changing weather, the unexpected encounters, and the enchantment that our islands offer.

Getting to the Isles of Scilly

Ahoy there, future island explorer! Let's talk about how to make your way to the treasured Isles of Scilly. It's a journey that promises awe-inspiring views, a touch of adventure, and a warm island welcome.

Setting Sail or Taking Flight

Your first stop will likely be the mainland of the UK. From there, you have a couple of options to reach our paradise. You can catch a short flight from several airports like Exeter, Newquay, or Land's End. The iconic Isles of Scilly Skybus (www.islesofscilly-travel.co.uk) is your own private magic carpet, whisking you over the sea to the islands.

Or, if you're feeling a bit more nautical, you can hop on a ferry from Penzance. The Scillonian III ferry (www.islesofscilly-travel.co.uk) journey on the waves takes about 2.5 to 3 hours, and it's a chance to soak in the ocean breeze, watch for seabirds, and maybe even spot a dolphin or two. The ferry is more than just transportation—it's the prelude to your island adventure.

Travel Tips for the Voyage

Now, here's a little local wisdom for you:

Ferry Finesse: If you're taking the ferry, make sure to book in advance, especially during peak seasons. The

Isles of Scilly Travel (www.islesofscilly-travel.co.uk) website is your go-to for schedules and reservations. And for those who are prone to seasickness, a trusty motion-sickness remedy might just be your new best friend.

Flight Delights: If you're opting for a flight, you're in for a treat. The aerial views of the islands are nothing short of spectacular. Snap some photos, or just gaze out the window and let the excitement build as you approach our shores. The Isles of Scilly Skybus offers a range of flights to choose from.

Island-Hopping Flights
Once you've reached the Isles, you might need to do a bit of island-hopping to get to your final destination. Tiny planes, known as "Skybus," will shuttle you between the islands. These flights are like a scenic tour, offering a bird's-eye view of the landscapes that you'll soon be exploring on foot.

Traveler's Note

Keep in mind that schedules might change due to weather conditions. Our maritime climate can be a bit whimsical, and safety always comes first. But don't worry, we locals are used to the ebb and flow of island life, and it's all part of the adventure.

So, whether you're soaring through the skies with Isles of Scilly Skybus or riding the waves with Scillonian III, getting to the Isles of Scilly is a journey to remember. Pack your anticipation, your sense of wonder, and a dash of flexibility, and you'll be well on your way to discovering the magic that our islands hold.

Navigating the Islands

Now that you've landed on the shores of the Isles of Scilly, let's chat about how to explore this exquisite archipelago. The Isles of Scilly might be small in size, but they're big on experiences. And lucky for you, getting around here is a breeze.

Walking on Sunshine

The most magical way to uncover the islands' charms? On foot, of course! Each island is a unique tapestry of landscapes, and wandering its paths is like diving into a storybook. Whether you're strolling along the sandy shores, trekking through moorland, or following coastal trails, your own two feet are your trusty steeds.

Two-Wheeled Adventures

Feeling a bit more adventurous? How about hopping on a bike? The islands are tailor-made for cycling, with quiet roads and stunning vistas around every bend. You can rent bikes from Adventure Scilly (www.adventurescilly.co.uk) and whether you're a leisurely rider or a more seasoned cyclist, the Isles' terrain has something for everyone.

Island Hopping Made Easy

Now, let's talk about moving between the islands. We've got something charmingly unique—the inter-island boats, locally known as "boatsmen." These boats are like the threads that weave our archipelago together, shuttling you between islands with ease. To catch a boatsman, head to the quays on each island where you'll find the boats waiting to ferry you across. They're not just transport; they're an integral part of island life, with skippers who know the tides and the winds like the back of their hands.

Sky-High Views

For those breathtaking vistas that make your heart skip a beat, take to the skies once again. The Isles of Scilly Skybus offers scenic flights between the islands, giving you a bird's-eye view of the landscapes you've explored and those waiting to be discovered. Check their schedules and book your flights at Isles of Scilly Travel (www.islesofscilly-travel.co.uk).

On Four Wheels: Buses and Cars

Ah, but there's more. While we treasure our pedestrian-friendly ways, you'll find limited bus services on the larger islands, especially St. Mary's. It's a convenient way to cover longer distances or simply take a leisurely ride around. And if you're looking for a touch of freedom, you can also rent a car from Europcar (0371

384 5975, www.europcar.co.uk, Rhino Car Hire (0845 508 9845, www.rhinocarhire.com or Enterprise Rent-A-Car Penzance (01736 332000, www.enterprise.co.uk) for a day of island exploration at your own pace.

Remember, everything here is on island time. Don't rush. Savor each moment, and let the gentle rhythm of the Isles guide your journey. Whether you're walking, cycling, boating, or flying, the beauty of the Isles of Scilly is that you're not just getting from point A to point B—you're weaving your own story into the fabric of this enchanting archipelago.

Chapter 3: Accommodation Guide

Choosing Your Island Base

Selecting the right island as your home away from home is a vital part of your Isles of Scilly experience. Each island has its distinct charm and offerings, catering to different preferences. Here's a brief overview to help you decide:

St. Mary's: The Heartbeat of the Isles

As the largest and most populated island, St. Mary's offers a range of accommodations and amenities. This makes it an excellent base if you prefer staying where the action is. You'll find hotels, inns, guesthouses, and self-catering options, allowing you to tailor your stay to your preferences. Additionally, St. Mary's is a hub for transportation, making it convenient for exploring other islands.

Tresco: Serenity Amidst Nature

For a more secluded and luxurious experience, Tresco is a popular choice. The island boasts elegant lodgings, offering a tranquil escape surrounded by nature's beauty. Tresco's proximity to the stunning Tresco Abbey Garden is a bonus for nature enthusiasts.

Bryher: Rustic Charm and Tranquility

If you're seeking a quiet and intimate setting, Bryher might be your haven. The island's cozy accommodations, tucked amidst unspoiled landscapes, provide a perfect backdrop for relaxation. Bryher's beaches and coastline are easily accessible for leisurely walks.

St. Martin's: Seaside Elegance

St. Martin's is synonymous with exquisite beaches and clear waters. This island is an ideal choice for those who wish to be close to nature while enjoying a touch of sophistication. Choose from accommodations that offer stunning sea views and easy access to the shoreline.

Remember, the right island base enhances your experience, providing not only a place to rest but also an integral part of your Isles of Scilly adventure.

Luxury Resorts and Boutique Hotels

Welcome to a realm where luxury meets the captivating beauty of the Isles of Scilly. If your heart seeks the finest comforts amidst nature's embrace, our selection of luxury resorts and boutique hotels will leave you enchanted.

Karma St. Martin's Hotel

Address: St. Martin's, Isles of Scilly, TR25 0QW
Website: https://karmagroup.com/find-destination/karma-retreats/karma-st-martins/

Nestled on the serene St. Martin's island, Karma St. Martin's Hotel invites you to experience opulence with a view. Overlooking azure waters and unspoiled landscapes, this haven seamlessly blends contemporary luxury with the island's tranquility. From elegant suites to lavish spa treatments, every detail is designed to cocoon you in comfort. Prepare for average pricing starting at $250 per night.

Hell Bay Hotel

Address: Bryher, Isles of Scilly, TR23 0PR
Website: www.hellbay.co.uk

Escape to the untamed beauty of Bryher and find solace at the Hell Bay Hotel. Perched on the rugged cliffs overlooking the Atlantic, this establishment epitomizes rustic elegance. Dine on sumptuous seafood, breathe in the salty sea breeze, and explore nearby attractions such as Hell Bay itself. Unwind in style, with an average rate of around $250 per night.

Star Castle Hotel

Address: Isles of Scilly TR21 0JA, United Kingdom

Website: www.star-castle.co.uk

St. Mary's harbors a gem in the form of Star Castle Hotel, a historic fortress turned luxury accommodation. The hotel exudes old-world charm and sophistication, offering superb views of the harbor. Delight in its gourmet dining and immerse yourself in the island's history. Prices for a night's stay range from $200 to $300.

Tregarthen's Hotel

Address: Garrison Hill, Isles of Scilly TR21 0PP, United Kingdom

Website: www.tregarthens-hotel.co.uk

For those who wish to be at the heart of St. Mary's bustling activity while enjoying luxury, Tregarthen's Hotel is a prime choice. Overlooking the historic harbor, this family-run hotel seamlessly blends comfort with convenience. Take leisurely walks along picturesque quays and immerse yourself in island life. Prices for a double room typically range from $150 to $200 per night.

Booking Tips

Advance Reservations: As these luxury accommodations are in high demand, it's wise to book well in advance, especially during peak seasons.

Indulgent Activities: Most luxury resorts offer a variety of upscale experiences, from fine dining to spa treatments. Inquire about packages and exclusive offerings upon booking.

Each of these luxury resorts and boutique hotels invites you to unwind and immerse yourself in a world where every detail is curated for your pleasure. Beyond the plush accommodations, you'll be surrounded by the natural allure of the Isles, beckoning you to explore its beauty.

Charming Bed and Breakfasts

Indulge in the warmth of island hospitality by choosing a charming bed and breakfast as your haven in the Isles of Scilly. These delightful accommodations not only provide comfort but also a personal touch that's quintessentially Scillonian.

Polreath Guest House

Address: Polreath Higher Town St. Martin's Isles of Scilly TR25 0QL, United Kingdom
Website: https://www.polreath.com/

Nestled in the heart of Hugh Town on St. Mary's, Polreath Guest House offers a cozy retreat with a friendly atmosphere. From hearty breakfasts to comfortable rooms, you'll find all the essentials for a pleasant stay. The bustling town and attractions like the Isles of Scilly Museum are just a stroll away. Prices for a double room start at approximately $100 per night.

The New Inn, Tresco

Address: New Grimsby, Hugh Town, United Kingdom, TR24 0QQ

Website: https://www.tresco.co.uk/staying/the-new-inn

The New Inn on Tresco presents an ideal setting to relax and immerse in island life. This charming establishment provides top-notch accommodations and delectable cuisine, situated at the heart of the island.

Prices commence from £185.00 per room, inclusive of breakfast.

Northwethel Guest House, St. Mary's

Address: 12 Pilot's Retreat, Isles of Scilly TR21 0PB, United Kingdom

Website: https://www.northwethelguesthouseislesofscilly.co.uk/

Northwethel Guest House in St. Mary's offers a cozy, family-operated B&B experience. Nestled in a tranquil cul-de-sac off Church Road, it provides spacious double or twin rooms with en-suite facilities. Amenities include tea and coffee provisions, TV, clock radio, WiFi, and towels. Pets are not allowed, and it's a non-smoking premise.

Rates start at £40.00 per person, including breakfast.

Crebinick House, St. Mary's

Address: Church St, Isles of Scilly TR21 0JT, United Kingdom
Website: https://www.crebinick.co.uk/

Crebinick House, located in Hugh Town on St. Mary's, boasts six en-suite guest rooms. This family-run B&B is just a brief stroll from the quay and two stunning beaches. Guests enjoy a daily offering of cold buffet and cooked breakfast.

Starting from £53.00 per person, breakfast is inclusive.

Rose Cottage, St. Mary's

Website: www.scillyrose.co.uk

Rose Cottage, overlooking the harbor in St. Mary's, stands as an en-suite harborside B&B. Every room provides captivating sea views, making it a prime location for accessing boats, beaches, dining, pubs, and shops. With a Four Star rating, Silver Award, and Breakfast Award, it offers free Wi-Fi.

Prices range from £50.00 to £65.00 per person, breakfast included.

Nancherrow, St. Mary's

Address: Pilot's Retreat, St Mary's TR21 0PB, United Kingdom

Nancherrow, on the outskirts of Hugh Town, St. Mary's, presents convenience and comfort. As a small, family-run B&B, Nancherrow offers en-suite double and twin-bedded accommodations.

Prices begin at £50.00 per person, with breakfast included.

Booking Tips
Personal Touch: Charming bed and breakfasts often offer personalized experiences, from local recommendations to homemade breakfasts. Engage with your hosts to make the most of your stay.

Local Insights: The hosts of these establishments are often long-time island residents who can provide valuable insights into the best hidden gems and lesser-known attractions.

Nurturing a Cozy Retreat

Each charming bed and breakfast offers a taste of island life and a haven where you can relax and recharge. The personalized attention and local insights will enrich your experience, ensuring your stay in the Isles of Scilly is nothing short of memorable.

Self-Catering Cottages and Rentals

Embrace the spirit of independence and immerse yourself in the island lifestyle by opting for self-catering cottages and rentals. These accommodations offer you the freedom to create your rhythm while basking in the beauty of the Isles of Scilly.

Isles of Scilly Cottages

Website: https://www.scillyselfcatering.com/

For a diverse selection of self-catering options across the islands, explore the site above. Choose from charming cottages, apartments, and houses that cater to different group sizes. Whether you seek a quaint hideaway or a family-friendly abode, these rentals offer the convenience of a home away from home. Average pricing varies widely based on the property, ranging from $100 to $300 per night.

Booking Tips

Grocery Essentials: As you'll be preparing your meals, it's advisable to stock up on groceries at local shops on the islands, ensuring you have everything you need.

Explore Local Fare: Don't miss the chance to sample local produce and seafood from the islands' markets and shops. Incorporating local flavors into your meals adds a delightful touch to your self-catering experience.

Self-catering cottages and rentals allow you to weave your own story in the Isles of Scilly. As you cook, relax, and gaze upon the vistas, you'll not only have a roof over your head but also a canvas upon which to paint your unique island memories.

Chapter 4: Exploring the Natural Beauty

Pristine Beaches and Coastal Marvels

Greetings, fellow wanderer, to the Isles of Scilly, a realm where nature's beauty thrives in every nook and cranny. Allow me to be your guide as we embark on a journey to discover the hidden treasures of pristine beaches and secluded coves that dot our picturesque archipelago.

Porthcressa Beach
Our voyage begins on St. Mary's, where Porthcressa Beach awaits, an oasis of tranquility just a stone's throw from Hugh Town. Feel the soft sand between your toes as you bask in the sun's warm embrace. This little haven offers a charming escape, perfect for a stroll or a moment of quiet reflection.

Rushy Bay

For those who yearn for isolation, St. Martin's is home to Rushy Bay, a haven accessible only by navigating a coastal path. The journey itself is an adventure, leading you to a secluded cove where the only sounds are the whispers of the wind and the gentle lapping of the waves. It's a spot to disconnect and immerse yourself in nature's embrace.

Great Bay

Venture to Bryher and uncover the untouched allure of Great Bay. Here, wild cliffs juxtapose against a serene sandy beach, providing a dramatic contrast. Whether arriving by boat or embarking on a scenic walk, you'll be greeted by the Atlantic's vastness and the island's untamed spirit.

Pelistry Bay

On St. Mary's, Pelistry Bay beckons with its unspoiled sands and ancient rock formations. This hidden gem offers a glimpse into the Isles of Scilly's geological history, and its tidal pools provide a playground for the curious and the adventurous. Observe seals lounging on the rocks as you lose yourself in the symphony of the sea.

Green Bay

Bryher's Green Bay beckons, where a stroll leads you to a cove embraced by rugged cliffs. The journey itself is an experience, and the reward is a crescent of soft sand nestled against crystalline waters. The seclusion of Green Bay invites you to revel in the solitude and reconnect with nature.

Periglis Beach

As we venture to St. Agnes, let Periglis Beach captivate your senses. A scenic walk unveils this hidden gem, where rock pools, white sands, and crystal-clear waters create an intimate setting for exploration. Seabirds dance overhead, and marine life thrives in the tidal pools, offering a glimpse into the wonders of island life.

Coastal Exploration Tips

Tides and Timing: Keep an eye on the tides, as some coves are only accessible during low tide. Plan your visits accordingly to fully enjoy their beauty.

Leave No Trace: As you venture into these untouched havens, remember to respect the environment. Leave no trace behind, ensuring the preservation of these natural wonders.

Pristine beaches and hidden coves are the Isles of Scilly's well-kept secrets. Each cove tells a story of untamed beauty, inviting you to step off the beaten path and into a world where the elements shape the landscape, and the symphony of nature plays on.

Nature Reserves and Wildlife Habitats

Ahoy, fellow adventurers, to the heart of the Isles of Scilly's untamed beauty! Our journey now takes us to the sacred realms of nature reserves and wildlife habitats, where the islands' flora and fauna flourish in harmony.

Join me as we unveil the enchantment of these sanctuaries.

Tresco Abbey Garden

Nestled on Tresco, the Tresco Abbey Garden stands as a horticultural masterpiece. Exotic plants from around the world thrive here, thanks to the mild climate. Wander through terraced landscapes, lush greenery, and vibrant blooms that paint a living canvas. Keep an eye out for red squirrels that scamper about, adding a touch of local charm.

Gugh and St. Agnes

As we sail to Gugh, which is connected to St. Agnes by a sandbar, prepare to witness a haven of nesting seabirds. This refuge is a treasure trove for ornithologists and nature enthusiasts. Be greeted by the cries of gulls and the sight of puffins along the cliffs—a symphony of island life that resonates deep within.

Bryher's Island Beauty

Bryher's Hillside Farm provides an insight into traditional island farming practices. Wander through lush pastures, discover ancient field systems, and catch sight of Shetland ponies that roam freely. This serene setting offers panoramic views, combining history and natural beauty in an embrace that's quintessentially Bryher.

St. Martin's Flora and Fauna

St. Martin's embraces its wildlife with open arms, and the diverse ecosystems here showcase the island's biodiversity. Explore the sandy shores and rocky shores that shelter marine life, while heathlands and grassy meadows offer habitats for ground-nesting birds. As you stroll, spot seals basking on the rocks, a testament to the island's commitment to preserving its treasures.

Lower Moors and Higher Moors

On St. Mary's, the Lower Moors and Higher Moors nature reserves are a testament to the islands' rich ecological diversity. Lower Moors, with its marshes and wetlands, is home to various bird species. Higher Moors is an ancient landscape with prehistoric relics and diverse flora. Together, they offer a glimpse into the Isles of Scilly's natural tapestry.

Wildlife Spotting Tips
Binoculars and Patience: To truly appreciate the wildlife, carry binoculars and embrace patience. Sometimes, nature's wonders reveal themselves when we least expect them.

Guided Tours: Join guided tours led by experts to gain deeper insights into the ecosystems and habits of the island's wildlife.

Nature reserves and wildlife habitats on the Isles of Scilly are a treasure trove of discovery. Each visit offers a chance to connect with the islands' delicate ecosystems, where every rustle in the underbrush and every soaring bird tells a story of the island's natural heritage.

Guided Birdwatching Tours

Ahoy, fellow bird enthusiasts and curious souls, as we embark on an avian adventure across the Isles of Scilly! Our archipelago is a haven for birdwatchers, where diverse habitats and a range of species converge in a symphony of feathered wonders. Join me as we spread our wings and explore the guided birdwatching tours that unveil the secrets of our skies.

Ornithological Delights Await
From March to October, our islands become a temporary residence for a plethora of migrating birds. The guides on these tours are not just experts but storytellers, weaving tales of the avian migrants who journey thousands of miles to our shores. They'll regale you with knowledge about the local ecology, behavior patterns, and conservation efforts that preserve these winged marvels.

Spotlight on Tours

Scilly Pelagics

Website: www.scillypelagics.com

Embark on a boat trip like no other with Scilly Pelagics. These tours venture offshore to the deep waters where pelagic species, including shearwaters, petrels, and skuas, are often spotted. The open ocean becomes your theater, with a naturalist guide sharing insights and spotting tips that bring these magnificent birds closer to your lens.

Scilly Walks

Website: www.scillywalks.co.uk

For those who prefer a terrestrial adventure, Scilly Walks offers guided birdwatching tours across the islands' diverse landscapes. From coastal cliffs to heathlands and wetlands, each habitat boasts its cast of avian characters. Binoculars in hand, you'll set off with a local guide who knows these islands like the back of their hand, ensuring you don't miss a single feathered friend.

Local Insights

Timing Matters: Different seasons bring different birds. Spring and autumn are prime migration times, while summer welcomes nesting species.

Be Respectful: While observing the birds, remember to maintain a respectful distance, keeping noise levels down to avoid disturbing their natural behavior.

Guided birdwatching tours offer a unique lens into the islands' biodiversity. As you venture along rugged coastlines or traverse heathlands alive with song, you'll discover a world of wings and melodies that add depth to your understanding of the Isles of Scilly's natural tapestry.

Gardens and Botanical Wonders

Greetings, fellow nature enthusiasts, as we embark on a journey that unveils the vibrant tapestry of gardens and botanical wonders on the Isles of Scilly. Here, the islands' temperate climate and fertile soil come together to create a canvas painted with an array of colors, scents, and textures. Join me as we step into the embrace of these living landscapes.

Tresco Abbey Garden

Our adventure begins on Tresco, home to the renowned Tresco Abbey Garden. This subtropical paradise is a living testament to the islands' unique climate. Wander along winding pathways, lined with exotic plants from around the world. Palms, succulents, and vibrant blooms thrive amidst ancient ruins, creating a juxtaposition of history and horticulture.

Abbey Garden
Website:
www.tresco.co.uk/enjoying/gardens/abbey-garden

Bella's Garden

In the heart of St. Mary's, Bella's Garden is a haven for plant lovers. This sheltered oasis, named after a local legend, is a sanctuary for native flora. Explore its meandering paths, rest in shaded corners, and discover a medley of local plants that have called the islands home for generations.

St. Mary's Hall Gardens

Nestled near Hugh Town, St. Mary's Hall Gardens is a hidden gem waiting to be explored. Discover a range of plants, from vibrant blooms to tranquil ponds that reflect the sky's hues. This tranquil space offers a chance to unwind amidst nature's symphony.

Trenoweth Nurseries

Tucked away on St. Martin's, Trenoweth Nurseries is more than a garden—it's a sanctuary for plant enthusiasts. Meander through a diverse collection of plants, many of which are grown here. The fragrant aromas and vivid colors make it a paradise for the senses.

Local Insights

Timing is Key: Gardens change with the seasons. Spring and early summer bring a burst of colors, while autumn offers a different palette as plants prepare for winter.

Guided Tours: Join guided garden tours for a deeper understanding of the plants, their history, and their significance to the islands.

Gardens and botanical wonders on the Isles of Scilly are a symphony of life, where every petal, leaf, and stem tells a story of the islands' natural splendor. As you explore these living landscapes, you're not merely observing; you're entering into a dialogue with nature itself.

Island Hiking Trails: Nature Walks and Scenic Views

Ahoy, fellow adventurers, and welcome to the untamed landscapes of the Isles of Scilly! Our journey now takes us along the well-worn paths of hiking trails, nature walks, and vantage points that offer a glimpse into the heart of our archipelago's natural beauty. Join me as we lace up our hiking boots and set forth on a voyage of discovery.

St. Mary's Circular Walk

Our first trail beckons on St. Mary's—the Circular Walk. This 6-mile loop offers a taste of the island's diverse landscapes. Meander along coastal cliffs, where the Atlantic's waves crash against ancient rocks. Traverse heathlands are alive with wildflowers, and pause at stunning viewpoints that reveal the islands' beauty from every angle.

Tresco's Castle Down Walk

On Tresco, Castle Down Walk is a journey through history and nature. As you ascend, the remains of an Iron Age hillfort come into view, a reminder of the island's ancient past. Reach the summit and be rewarded with panoramic views, where azure waters stretch to meet the horizon, and neighboring islands seem within arm's reach.

St. Agnes Coastal Path

St. Agnes offers a coastal path that's a visual feast for the senses. Wander along dramatic cliffs that drop to secluded coves and hidden beaches. Keep an eye out for seals basking on the rocks below, a sight that adds a touch of magic to your hike. The trail is a testament to the islands' rugged allure and the harmony between land and sea.

Bryher's Island Odyssey
Bryher invites you to an island odyssey, with trails that traverse its lush landscapes. Journey through fragrant heathlands, where the calls of seabirds accompany your steps. Reach vantage points that offer sweeping views of neighboring islands, each frame a masterpiece of nature's craftsmanship.

Local Insights
Sturdy Footwear: Hiking trails can vary in terrain. Sturdy footwear and appropriate clothing ensure you're prepared for your adventure.

Pack Essentials: Carry water, snacks, a map, and perhaps a pair of binoculars to fully appreciate the scenery and wildlife.

Hiking trails, nature walks, and scenic viewpoints on the Isles of Scilly are more than routes; they're tales waiting to be told. Each step leads to a new vista, a fresh perspective, and an opportunity to connect with the islands' untamed spirit.

Chapter 5: Island Adventures

Water Sports and Aquatic Activities

Ahoy, fellow water enthusiasts, as we set sail into the heart of aquatic adventures on the Isles of Scilly! Here, the boundless azure waters are our playground, inviting us to embrace the thrill of water sports and immerse ourselves in the beauty of the Atlantic. Join me as we dip our toes into an ocean of possibilities.

Kayaking and Paddleboarding
Grab your paddle and hop into a kayak or onto a paddleboard—the perfect way to explore the islands' coastline at your own pace. Glide over the gentle waves, discovering hidden coves, rocky outcrops, and sea caves. Kayaks and paddleboards are available for rent from various providers, and you can set off from beaches like Porthcressa Beach on St. Mary's or Rushy Bay on St. Martin's. Rental fees vary depending on the duration of use.

Sailing Adventures

Set sail and harness the winds that sweep across our archipelago. Whether you're an experienced sailor or a curious novice, there's a vessel waiting to carry you into the Atlantic's embrace. Charter boats are available for sailing adventures, and the island of Tresco is a popular starting point. Companies like Scilly Sailing offer guided sailing trips that provide both the equipment and the expertise to ensure a safe and enjoyable experience.

Snorkeling and Diving

Dive beneath the surface and unveil a world teeming with marine life. Snorkeling and diving allow you to explore underwater realms, where vibrant fish dart among rocky reefs and kelp forests. Breathtaking snorkeling spots include Porthcressa Beach on St. Mary's and Par Beach on St. Martin's. For diving, Scilly Diving offers guided trips to explore the islands' underwater wonders. Rental equipment and guided dives come at a fee.

Wild Swimming

For the adventurous at heart, wild swimming offers an unscripted connection with the sea. Slip into the refreshing waters of secluded coves, allowing the waves to cradle you as you revel in the sense of liberation that only the open sea can provide. There's no fee for wild swimming—just a daring spirit and a love for the ocean.

Local Insights

Safety First: Always prioritize safety. Check weather conditions and tides before embarking on any water activity.

Guided Experiences: If you're new to water sports, consider joining guided sessions led by local experts. They'll provide not only equipment but also insights into the best spots and techniques.

Water sports and aquatic activities on the Isles of Scilly are more than adrenaline rushes; they're invitations to connect with the ocean's rhythm and the islands' maritime spirit. Each wave you ride and each stroke you take becomes a conversation with the sea itself.

Biking Trails and Cycling Routes

Hello, fellow adventurers and cycling enthusiasts, as we embark on an island expedition that's best experienced on two wheels! The Isles of Scilly offer a cyclist's paradise—a network of biking trails and cycling routes that wind through our picturesque landscapes. Join me as we saddle up and explore the archipelago's beauty at our own pace.

St. Mary's Circular Route
Our journey begins with the St. Mary's Circular Route, a perfect introduction to the island's charm. The 10-mile loop takes you through coastal paths, quaint villages, and historical landmarks. Pedal past sandy shores, where the waves serenade your ride, and pause at viewpoints that offer panoramic vistas of the surrounding sea.

Tresco's Hidden Gems
Tresco beckons with biking trails that traverse the island's hidden gems. Explore the Abbey Garden, Castle Down, and quiet lanes that wind through serene

landscapes. Cycling on Tresco is a journey of discovery, where every twist and turn unveils a new facet of the island's natural beauty.

St. Martin's Coastal Ride

St. Martin's boasts a coastal ride that's a visual feast for cyclists. Pedal along paths that hug the shoreline, providing glimpses of azure waters and secluded beaches. The gentle inclines and stunning views make this route a favorite among those seeking both adventure and tranquility.

Bryher's Lanes and Byways

Bryher's lanes and byways invite cyclists to embrace the island's rugged allure. Wind through heathlands adorned with wildflowers and cycle to vantage points that offer sweeping views of neighboring islands. With its diverse landscapes, Bryher offers trails for both leisurely rides and exhilarating adventures.

Local Insights

Bike Rentals: Rentals are available on the islands, allowing you to choose from traditional bicycles, electric bikes, and even tandems for a shared adventure.

Trail Difficulty: Trails vary in difficulty, from leisurely rides suitable for families to more challenging routes for experienced cyclists.

Biking trails and cycling routes on the Isles of Scilly aren't just a means of transportation; they're a passport to the islands' soul. Each pedal stroke carries you through history, nature, and the rhythms of island life.

Historical Sites and Landmarks

Greetings, curious souls and history enthusiasts, as we embark on a journey through time across the Isles of Scilly! Our archipelago is steeped in stories of ages past, and within its embrace lie historical sites and landmarks that offer glimpses into the tapestry of our island's heritage. Join me as we walk in the footsteps of those who came before, unraveling the tales etched into our landscape.

Garrison Walls of Star Castle

Our voyage into history commences at Star Castle on St. Mary's, a fortress dating back to the 16th century. The garrison walls whisper tales of battles, sieges, and the resilience of those who once defended the islands. As you explore its corridors and ramparts, you're transported to a time when the islands were a strategic stronghold.

Old Town Church

The Old Town Church on St. Mary's stands as a serene sentinel of the past. Its ancient walls hold echoes of generations who sought solace within its confines. Inside, discover intricate stained glass windows, weathered gravestones, and an atmosphere that's both reverent and contemplative.

Gugh's Cromwell's Castle

A short stroll across the sandbar from St. Agnes leads you to the isle of Gugh, where Cromwell's Castle awaits.

This coastal fortress, built during the English Civil War, offers sweeping views of the sea and neighboring islands. As you explore its chambers and gaze through arrow slits, you're transported to a time of conflict and conquest.

St. Martin's Daymark

St. Martin's Daymark is a beacon of history, guiding ships through treacherous waters for centuries. This towering structure served as a navigational aid for sailors, and today, it stands as a testament to the islands' maritime past. Ascend to the top for panoramic views, and let the wind carry whispers of mariners who relied on this landmark.

Harry's Walls

On Bryher, the ruins of Harry's Walls tell a tale of resilience and protection. This ancient fortification dates back to the Iron Age and offers a glimpse into the island's prehistoric past. Explore the remains of walls that once stood as a shield against invaders, and imagine life in an era untouched by modernity.

Buzza Tower

Perched on a hilltop on St. Mary's, Buzza Tower stands as an architectural treasure. Originally constructed as a windmill, it was later converted into a watchtower during World War II. Climb to its pinnacle for panoramic views that encompass both land and sea, and reflect on the generations who relied on this vantage point.

Local Insights

Guided Tours: Join guided tours to gain insights into the history of these sites, unraveling the stories that might be missed at first glance.

Interactive Exhibits: Some historical sites, like the Isles of Scilly Museum on St. Mary's, feature interactive exhibits that dive deeper into the islands' past.

Historical sites and landmarks on the Isles of Scilly are more than relics; they're windows into a bygone era. With every stone you touch and every story you hear, you're forging a connection with the generations who shaped our islands.

Lighthouses and Maritime History

Ahoy, maritime enthusiasts and seekers of seafaring tales, as we set sail on a maritime odyssey through the Isles of Scilly! Our archipelago's history is interwoven with the sea, and its lighthouses stand as beacons that have guided mariners through tempestuous waters. Join me as we explore these towering sentinels and unravel the maritime stories that have shaped our islands.

St. Agnes Lighthouse
Our journey commences on St. Agnes, where the St. Agnes Lighthouse stands resolute against the elements. This iconic tower has safeguarded sailors for over a century, its light piercing the night to guide ships to safety. Explore the lighthouse grounds, where historical displays and artifacts offer a glimpse into the lives of those who tended the light.

Bishop Rock Lighthouse

The Bishop Rock Lighthouse, perched upon treacherous rocks off the western coast, is a testament to human ingenuity and courage. This lighthouse, one of the world's most isolated, endures the fury of the Atlantic, a symbol of unwavering determination to keep sailors safe. While a visit to the lighthouse itself is not possible due to its location, boat trips offer a chance to marvel at its architectural marvel from afar.

Tales of Resilience

Maritime history on the Isles of Scilly is alive with stories of shipwrecks, heroic rescues, and the symbiotic relationship between islanders and the sea. The remains of shipwrecks, such as the Cita, evoke tales of storms and survival, while the Valhalla Collection on Bryher offers a treasure trove of artifacts salvaged from maritime tragedies.

Local Insights

Lighthouse Tours: Join guided tours of St. Agnes Lighthouse to gain insights into its history, operation, and the lives of its keepers.

Maritime Museums: Explore the Isles of Scilly Museum on St. Mary's for exhibits that delve into the islands' maritime heritage, from shipwrecks to maritime crafts.

Lighthouses and maritime history on the Isles of Scilly are more than stories—they're threads that weave together the islanders' lives and the rhythms of the sea. As you stand beside these beacons of light, you're not just witnessing history; you're becoming a part of it.

Unique Experiences: From Boat Tours to Rock Climbing

Greetings, fellow adventurers and thrill-seekers, as we delve into the world of unique experiences that await on the Isles of Scilly! Our archipelago is a canvas of possibilities, offering everything from serene boat tours that navigate azure waters to exhilarating rock climbing that defies gravity. Join me as we step outside the ordinary and embrace the extraordinary.

Guided Boat Tours

Our journey begins on the water, where guided boat tours invite you to explore the islands from a maritime perspective. Embark on an expedition with SeaQuest Scilly (https://www.seaquestscilly.com/) or the Island Sea Safaris (www.islandseasafaris.co.uk), unveiling hidden coves, rugged cliffs, and secluded beaches accessible only by sea. Prices typically range from $30 to $50 per person, depending on the tour duration.

Kayak Adventures

For those seeking a more intimate connection with the sea, kayak adventures are a revelation. Book a guided kayak tour with Scilly Seal Snorkelling and Wildlife Safaris (www.scillysealsnorkelling.com) or Ocean High (www.oceanhigh.co.uk) and paddle through crystalline waters, gliding past rocky outcrops and glistening sands. Prices for guided kayak tours start at around $40 per person.

Rock Climbing Thrills

Feel the pulse of adventure as you conquer the cliffs that guard our shores. For rock climbing enthusiasts, Adventure Scilly (www.adventurescilly.co.uk) offers guided climbing experiences tailored to various skill levels. Whether you're a seasoned climber or a newcomer to the sport, prices for rock climbing adventures begin at approximately $50 per person.

Local Insights

Guided Expeditions: For safety and a deeper understanding of these unique adventures, consider joining guided expeditions led by local experts.

Equipment and Training: Whether it's boat tours, kayaking, or rock climbing, equipment and training are readily available, ensuring both safety and an enriching experience.

Unique experiences on the Isles of Scilly are like chapters waiting to be written in the book of your journey. Each moment spent on a kayak, scaling a cliff, or cruising the waves becomes part of the narrative—a tale you'll share and treasure for years to come.

Chapter 6: Embracing Island Culture

Engaging with Islanders

Greetings, fellow explorers, as we step beyond the surface and delve into the heart of island life—the warmth of its people. Engaging with the locals is a treasure trove of cultural immersion, and on the Isles of Scilly, our communities extend a heartfelt invitation to share in their stories, traditions, and way of life. Join me as we discover the art of connecting with the heart and soul of the islands.

Community Spirit
Our journey into island culture begins with the people who call the Isles of Scilly home. Islanders are known for their friendliness and welcoming nature, always eager to share insights about their island paradise. From the shopkeepers who greet you with a smile to the

fishermen who spin tales of the sea, engaging with locals unveils layers of authenticity beyond the guidebooks.

Visiting Local Establishments

Step into local pubs, cafés, and shops—these are the heartbeats of island life. Strike up a conversation with the barista as you savor your morning coffee, ask the bartender for recommendations on local brews, or chat with artisans about their crafts. You'll find that these interactions offer not just information, but a sense of camaraderie that bridges the gap between visitor and resident.

Participating in Events

Embracing island culture is also about participating in local events and celebrations. Whether it's a village fête, a traditional dance, or a harvest festival, joining these festivities allows you to experience the islands as an insider. The Isles of Scilly are dotted with events throughout the year, and each offers a unique opportunity to immerse yourself in the island's rhythms.

Local Insights

Openness and Respect: Approach interactions with openness and respect, valuing the perspectives and stories that locals have to share.

Ask and Listen: Don't hesitate to ask questions and listen attentively to the responses. Islanders are often eager to share their experiences and insights.

Engaging with Islanders isn't just about learning; it's about forming connections that enrich your experience. Each interaction, whether a friendly chat at a local market or a shared laugh at a village event, becomes a brushstroke in the canvas of your island journey.

Local Etiquette and Customs

Greetings, curious travelers, as we step into the realm of island culture—one that's rich with traditions and customs that shape the way of life on the Isles of Scilly. Engaging with locals isn't just about making connections; it's about respecting and understanding the customs that define our community. Join me as we delve into the tapestry of local etiquette, allowing you to navigate our islands with grace and appreciation.

A Warm Greeting

Island etiquette begins with a warm and genuine greeting. When entering a shop, café, or any establishment, it's customary to offer a friendly "hello" or "good morning." A simple smile and a nod can go a long way in establishing a positive connection with locals.

Respecting Personal Space

While our islands may be close-knit, respecting personal space is an essential aspect of local etiquette. Islanders value their space, so be mindful of maintaining a comfortable distance in public places. Politeness and consideration are the cornerstones of harmonious interactions.

Cultural Awareness

Taking the time to learn about local customs can be a bridge to deeper connections. For example, if invited into someone's home, it's a thoughtful gesture to bring a small gift, such as a local treat or a bottle of wine. Learning a few phrases in the local dialect, such as "konnichiwa" (hello) in Cornish, showcases your appreciation for the culture.

Paying It Forward

A gesture as simple as holding the door for someone, offering your seat to an elder on the bus, or helping a fellow visitor with directions embodies the spirit of our community. Acts of kindness and consideration are a universal language that transcends cultural differences.

Local Insights

Observe and Learn: Observe how locals interact with each other and follow their lead when it comes to greetings and social cues.

Tread Lightly: When participating in local events or celebrations, be respectful of the customs and traditions that shape these occasions.

Understanding local etiquette and customs is a way of paying homage to the tapestry of our community. By respecting these norms, you're not just a traveler passing through; you're an honorary islander, leaving footprints of appreciation and understanding in your wake.

Festivals and Events

Ahoy, fellow adventurers, as we dive into the vibrant tapestry of island life—a world woven with festivals and events that pulse to the rhythm of the Isles of Scilly. Our archipelago isn't just a scenic paradise; it's also a stage for celebrations that illuminate the heart and soul of our community. Join me as we embark on a journey through time, where festivals are threads that connect us to the past, present, and future.

From the moment you step onto our shores, you're invited to partake in a calendar brimming with festivities. Each season brings its own unique events, reflecting the changing landscapes and the spirit of the islanders. Whether it's a traditional fête, a music festival, or a nautical regatta, these gatherings showcase the island's vibrancy.

Bryher's Pirate Day

Ahoy, matey! Bryher's Pirate Day is a swashbuckling extravaganza that transforms the island into a pirate's paradise. Join the festivities as locals and visitors don pirate attire, take part in treasure hunts, and enjoy live entertainment. This family-friendly event is usually free to attend, offering a touch of whimsy to your island experience.

Tresco Abbey Garden's Garden Party

Tresco Abbey Garden hosts an annual Garden Party on August 5th that's a feast for the senses. Against the backdrop of blooming flora, revel in live music, delectable treats, and a convivial atmosphere. Engage with fellow visitors and locals while celebrating the island's botanical wonders.

Tickets: £35 for adults, £15 for children (ages 5-15) and free for children under 5

Low Tide Day

An exploration of the islands' culture wouldn't be complete without participating in Low Tide Day on St. Martin's, which will take place on September 1st. This unique event reveals hidden treasures as the tide recedes, creating temporary pathways between islets. Join guided walks, uncover marine life, and experience a true connection with the ebb and flow of the sea. Low Tide Day is usually free to attend.

The Creative Scilly Festival

The Creative Scilly Festival runs from the 12th to the 20th of May and includes a weekend Festival of Nature in collaboration with the Isles of Scilly Wildlife Trust. The festival will include a variety of live theater, music, and film performances, as well as open studios and workshops. Highlights include celebrated singer/songwriter Angeline Morrison, Ha Hum Ah Theatre, an evening with novelist and photographer David R Abram, and another chance to watch St Mary's Theatre Club's sell-out Bishop Rock Lighthouse performance.

Taste of Scilly Food Festival

Indulge your taste buds in the Taste of Scilly Food Festival, spanning from September 15th to 24th. This delectable event showcases the islands' culinary delights, with local produce, seafood feasts, and cooking demonstrations that reveal the flavors of our archipelago. While some events might be free, others could have a nominal fee associated.

Local Insights

Plan Ahead: Research the dates of upcoming festivals and events to align your visit with these enriching experiences.

Participate with Gusto: Don't be shy about joining in the festivities, as many events are open to both locals and visitors alike.

Festivals and events on the Isles of Scilly aren't just opportunities for merriment; they're windows into the soul of our community. As you revel in the music, laughter, and camaraderie, you're not just an observer—you're a participant in a timeless tradition that links the past, present, and future.

Local Arts and Crafts Traditions

Greetings, fellow enthusiasts of island life, as we step into the realm of creativity and craftsmanship that define the spirit of the Isles of Scilly. Our archipelago isn't just a paradise of natural beauty; it's also a haven for artisans who channel their talents into exquisite works of art. Join me as we explore the world of local arts and crafts, where tradition and innovation intertwine to create treasures that embody the essence of our islands.

Craftsmanship that Tells Stories

The artistry of the Isles of Scilly is a reflection of its history, culture, and landscape. From the brushstrokes of painters capturing the play of light on the sea to the intricate details of handmade jewelry inspired by marine life, each creation is a narrative that speaks of the island's soul.

Sea-Inspired Art

With the sea as our constant companion, it's no wonder that the ocean finds its way into the heart of local art. Discover stunning seascapes, sculptures, and jewelry that pay homage to the marine world. Gaze upon a canvas that transports you to sunsets over the water, or adorn yourself with jewelry reminiscent of the treasures washed ashore.

Pottery and Ceramics

Explore the world of pottery and ceramics that reflect the rugged beauty of the Isles of Scilly. Visit local studios where skilled artisans shape clay into functional pieces and decorative works. From handmade mugs that cradle your morning brew to elegant bowls that grace your dining table, these creations are both art and everyday indulgence.

Textiles and Wearable Art
Uncover textiles that bear the imprint of island life. Handwoven scarves, clothing adorned with island-inspired motifs, and accessories that capture the essence of the sea—all invite you to embrace the islands even when you're far from their shores.

Local Insights
Meet the Artisans: Visit local studios and workshops to witness the creative process firsthand and interact with the talented artisans.

Souvenirs with a Story: When you bring home a piece of local art, you're not just acquiring an item; you're taking home a piece of the island's history and culture.

Local arts and crafts traditions are a doorway to a world of imagination and ingenuity. Whether you're seeking a keepsake to remember your island journey or a unique gift that captures the spirit of our community, these creations are more than objects—they're embodiments of the Isle of Scilly's enduring allure.

Visiting Museums and Cultural Centers

Greetings, fellow seekers of cultural treasures, as we embark on a journey into the heart of the Isles of Scilly—a realm where history, art, and tradition converge to create a tapestry of heritage. Our archipelago isn't just a sanctuary of natural wonders; it's also a haven for those yearning to delve into the stories that shaped our community. Join me as we explore the museums and cultural centers that offer a glimpse into the soul of the islands.

Discovering Island Narratives
Museums and cultural centers on the Isles of Scilly aren't just repositories of artifacts; they're gateways to understanding our past, present, and the intricate tapestry that binds them. These institutions invite you to immerse

yourself in the island's rich heritage, revealing stories that span centuries.

Tresco Abbey Garden Valhalla Collection
Nestled within the Tresco Abbey Garden, the Valhalla Collection transports you to the maritime history of our islands. The collection comprises intricately carved figureheads salvaged from shipwrecks, each with a tale to tell. Wander among these wooden figures, and you'll sense the maritime spirit that has long coursed through our veins. Entry to the Valhalla Collection is usually included with the admission fee to Tresco Abbey Garden.

The Isles of Scilly Museum
Located on St. Mary's, the Isles of Scilly Museum stands as a portal to the past. Step inside to uncover a trove of historical artifacts, photographs, and documents that unveil the lives of those who called these islands home. From tales of shipwrecks to the legacy of islanders, this museum paints a vivid portrait of our community's evolution. Admission to the Isles of Scilly Museum is

usually free, though donations are often appreciated to support the museum's preservation efforts.

Phoenix Craft Workshops

Aspiring artists and those with a passion for craftsmanship will find solace in the Phoenix Craft Workshops. Here, you can witness artisans at work, creating pottery, jewelry, and textiles that draw inspiration from the islands. Engage with the artists, learn about their techniques, and perhaps even create your own masterpiece. The workshops may have a nominal fee, but the experience is worth every penny for those seeking hands-on engagement.

Local Insights

Curiosity as Your Guide: Approach each museum and cultural center with an open heart and inquisitive mind, as you're about to unveil the layers of our island's narrative.

Interactive Experiences: Some centers offer workshops and hands-on activities, allowing you to truly immerse yourself in the creative process.

Visiting museums and cultural centers on the Isles of Scilly is more than an excursion; it's a journey through time. As you step into these spaces, you're not just an observer; you're a time traveler, connecting with the stories, art, and heritage that have shaped our island community.

Chapter 7: Gastronomic Delights: Dining on the Isles

Island Flavors: A Culinary Introduction

Greetings, fellow food explorers, as we embark on a delectable journey through the heart of the Isles of Scilly—a realm where flavors are as diverse as the landscapes that surround us. Our archipelago isn't just a paradise for the eyes; it's also a haven for your taste buds, offering a medley of culinary experiences that celebrate the bounty of land and sea. Join me as we dive into the world of island flavors, where each dish tells a story of our community's connection to nature and tradition.

A Symphony of Island Ingredients
The Isles of Scilly are blessed with a cornucopia of fresh, locally sourced ingredients that form the foundation of our cuisine. From succulent seafood harvested from the surrounding waters to the vibrant

produce nurtured by our fertile soil, every bite encapsulates the essence of island life.

Seafood Sensations

Our relationship with the sea is profound, and it's reflected in our dishes. Indulge in freshly caught crab, lobster, and succulent scallops, prepared with a delicate touch to let the natural flavors shine through. Sample the iconic "Stargazy Pie," where fish heads peer up from a golden crust, paying homage to the fishing heritage that sustains our community.

Garden Delights

Local gardens and allotments yield an abundance of vegetables that grace our plates. Savor the sweetness of island-grown tomatoes, the crispness of freshly picked greens, and the earthy notes of root vegetables that flourish in our temperate climate. These ingredients star in salads, sides, and even hearty soups that warm the soul.

Traditional Recipes, Modern Twists

While honoring tradition, our island chefs infuse contemporary creativity into their culinary endeavors. Enjoy classic Cornish pasties filled with local meats and vegetables, or relish a fusion of flavors in dishes that celebrate global influences while using the finest island ingredients.

Local Insights

Farmers' Markets: Engage with the island's culinary culture by visiting farmers' markets, where you can meet local producers and sample their creations.

Seasonal Delights: Our cuisine follows the rhythm of nature, with seasonal specialties that reflect the changing harvests.

Dining on the Isles of Scilly isn't just about filling your stomach; it's about embracing a way of life that's intimately connected to nature and community. As you savor each bite, you're not just indulging in food—you're partaking in a story that's been written by generations of islanders, etching their love for the land and sea into every dish.

Local Cuisine and Seafood Specialties

Ahoy, fellow epicureans, as we set sail on a culinary adventure that explores the heart of the Isles of Scilly—a realm where every bite is a symphony of flavors, a celebration of the land and sea that surround us. Our archipelago isn't just a visual wonder; it's a haven for food enthusiasts, offering a tapestry of local dishes that pay homage to our maritime heritage. Join me as we embark on a journey through our island's cuisine, where traditional flavors and seafood specialties take center stage.

An Oceanic Overture
The sea is our lifeline, and its bounties grace our plates in the most delightful ways. From the rhythmic lapping of waves to the aroma of freshly cooked seafood, every element of island life is intertwined with the ocean's embrace.

Seafood Sensations

Prepare to be dazzled by the seafood delights that define our culinary identity. Indulge in succulent crab, where the sweet and tender meat is lovingly extracted and showcased in salads or sandwiches. Delve into the rich flavors of freshly caught lobster, a true luxury that our island's waters provide. And don't miss the chance to relish scallops, seared to perfection and served with a touch of island flair.

Traditional Fare

Our local cuisine isn't just a collection of ingredients; it's a reflection of our history and way of life. Taste the flavors of tradition in dishes like "Stargazy Pie," a quirky yet beloved creation where fish heads peek out from a golden pastry crust. Savor the robust goodness of Cornish pasties, filled with island-grown vegetables and tender meats, offering a satisfying and portable meal for your island explorations.

Island-to-Table Philosophy

Our island-to-table philosophy isn't just a trend—it's a way of life. Engage in the joy of dining on ingredients that are often sourced just steps away from where you sit. Feel the connection to the land and sea as you savor dishes crafted with love and care by our local chefs.

Local Insights

Meet the Fishermen: Engage with the local fishing community and learn about their sustainable practices, which ensure the health of our oceans for generations to come.

Farm-to-Table Delights: Look for restaurants and eateries that proudly showcase locally sourced ingredients, giving you an authentic taste of the islands.

Dining on the Isles of Scilly isn't just a meal—it's an experience that immerses you in our community's history, culture, and love for the sea. As you savor each bite of seafood and traditional dishes, you're not just indulging in food; you're engaging in a culinary voyage that speaks to the very heart of our archipelago.

Dining Establishments Overview

Ahoy, fellow food enthusiasts, as we set sail on a gastronomic journey that uncovers the diverse dining landscape of the Isles of Scilly—a realm where each meal is a celebration of our island's bounty. Our archipelago isn't just a scenic paradise; it's a haven for culinary adventurers seeking an array of dining experiences that reflect our community's spirit. Join me as we navigate the culinary map and discover the dining establishments that cater to every palate and craving.

Eateries that Echo the Sea

From casual beachside cafes to charming restaurants overlooking the harbor, the dining scene on the Isles of Scilly is as diverse as the ocean itself. While each establishment has its unique ambiance, they all share a common ingredient—our island's connection to the sea.

Seaside Cafés and Quaint Pubs

Feel the sand between your toes as you dine in one of the beachfront cafés that offer panoramic views of the ocean.

Savor hearty breakfasts, light lunches, and island-inspired dishes made from locally sourced ingredients. For a relaxing beachfront meal, consider visiting Juliet's Garden Café (www.julietsgardenrestaurant.co.uk) or The Beach Restaurant (https://scillybeach.com/beach/), both offering a delightful blend of flavors and coastal vistas.

If you're seeking the charm of a traditional pub, you won't be disappointed. Many of our local pubs offer classic pub fare along with a selection of ales that have been brewed with care. Check out The Mermaid Inn (www.mermaidscilly.co.uk) or The Atlantic Inn (https://atlanticinnscilly.co.uk/) for an authentic pub experience with a touch of island warmth.

Harbor-Side Dining

Imagine indulging in a sumptuous meal while gazing out at the bustling harbor. Many of our dining establishments offer this perfect pairing, allowing you to watch boats dance on the water as you savor dishes that celebrate both land and sea. Fresh seafood takes center stage here, with menus that highlight the catch of the day and showcase the culinary creativity of our local chefs. The Flying Boat Café and Dibble & Grub (https://www.dibbleandgrub.co.uk/) are wonderful options for harbor-side dining, offering an inviting ambiance and delectable coastal-inspired fare.

Fine Dining with an Island Twist

For those seeking a more refined experience, the Isles of Scilly have you covered. Discover restaurants that fuse the elegance of fine dining with the flavors of our islands. Prepare to be tantalized by tasting menus that spotlight local ingredients prepared with a masterful touch. The Ruin Beach Café (https://www.tresco.co.uk/eating/ruin-cafe) and The Beach Restaurant offer exceptional fine dining experiences, where each dish is a work of art celebrating our island's essence.

Local Insights

Reservations are Your Friend: Since the island's dining scene can be intimate, it's a good idea to make reservations, especially during peak tourist seasons.

Seek Out Island Specialties: Don't miss the opportunity to sample dishes that reflect our maritime heritage, from freshly caught seafood to traditional island recipes.

Dining on the Isles of Scilly isn't just about satiating your hunger; it's about immersing yourself in our community's culture and flavors. As you enjoy meals that showcase the best of land and sea, you're not just indulging in cuisine; you're engaging in an experience that connects you to our archipelago's soul.

Chapter 8: Relaxation and Wellness

Spa and Wellness Retreats

Ahoy, seekers of tranquility and rejuvenation, as we embark on a voyage that embraces the serenity and healing power of the Isles of Scilly—a realm where relaxation and wellness intertwine with the gentle lull of the sea. Our archipelago isn't just a visual paradise; it's a sanctuary for those yearning to escape the stresses of modern life. Join me as we delve into the realm of spa and wellness retreats, where nature's embrace merges with expert care to restore your body and soul.

Healing in Harmony with Nature
The Isles of Scilly, with their unspoiled beauty and therapeutic ambiance, provide the perfect backdrop for an immersive wellness experience. Picture yourself cocooned in a world of tranquility, where the soothing

sounds of the sea and the gentle caress of the breeze meld with the practiced hands of skilled therapists.

Seaside Sanctuaries

Explore spas and wellness retreats that are nestled in perfect harmony with the island's natural surroundings. Enveloped by the calming aura of the ocean, you'll find solace in treatments that draw from the sea's bounty, utilizing mineral-rich seaweed and salt to detoxify and replenish.

One such haven of rejuvenation is the Karma St. Martin's Spa (www.karmagroup.com/find-destination/karma-st-martins), where wellness rituals inspired by our island's ethos await you. For a truly serene experience, immerse yourself in therapies at the Tresco Island Spa (https://www.tresco.co.uk/enjoying/spa) located on Tresco Island.

Holistic Therapies

Uncover a world of holistic therapies that reflect the island's ethos of holistic living. Engage in yoga sessions that salute the rising sun, allowing your body to stretch and your mind to find balance. Indulge in meditation sessions that offer respite from the daily grind, inviting you to connect with the present moment.

Tailored Experiences

Wellness retreats on the Isles of Scilly understand that each individual's needs are unique. Many offer personalized experiences that cater to your preferences and desired outcomes. Whether it's a restorative massage, a facial using local botanicals, or a full-body treatment that employs the power of essential oils, your well-being is at the heart of every session.

Local Insights

Booking Ahead: As these wellness retreats offer a limited number of spots to ensure an intimate experience, it's advisable to book your sessions in advance.

Connect with Nature: Let the island's natural beauty enhance your wellness journey. Take leisurely walks along the shore after a treatment or find a quiet spot to meditate and absorb the tranquility.

Partaking in a spa and wellness retreat on the Isles of Scilly isn't merely about indulgence; it's about embracing a holistic experience that unites your inner and outer worlds. As you surrender to the healing touch of the therapies and the peaceful rhythm of the island, you're not just pampering yourself; you're embarking on a journey of self-care that honors the tie between body, mind, and spirit.

Yoga and Meditation Escapes

Ahoy, fellow seekers of serenity and inner harmony, as we embark on a voyage to the heart of tranquility on the Isles of Scilly—a realm where the rhythm of the waves becomes the backdrop to your soul's journey. Our archipelago isn't just a picturesque escape; it's a sanctuary for those who yearn to align their spirits with the gentle cadence of the sea. Join me as we explore the realm of yoga and meditation escapes, where the islands' embrace nurtures both body and soul.

Unveiling the Inner Landscape

Imagine the morning sun casting its gentle glow on the shore as you engage in yoga poses that echo the island's serenity. Or picture yourself nestled in a quiet nook, surrounded by nature's embrace, as you dive into the depths of meditation. These escapes aren't just activities; they're gateways to the sanctuary within.

Yoga Amidst Nature

The Isles of Scilly offer a canvas of natural beauty for your yoga journey. Imagine the ethereal beauty of Porthcressa Beach (www.visitislesofscilly.com/explore/things-to-do/activities/yoga-pilates), where yoga sessions are held against the backdrop of the shimmering sea. Breathe in the healing energy of the ocean breeze as you stretch and align your body with the soothing sounds of the waves.

Meditation Retreats

Engage in meditation escapes that transport you to a realm of inner quietude. Whether you choose a guided meditation on the beach or a silent meditation amidst lush gardens, you'll find your soul resonating with the island's tranquil vibrations.

Holistic Connection

Yoga and meditation are more than physical practices; they're paths to a holistic connection. Unplug from the distractions of daily life and embrace the island's serene ambiance, allowing your body to align with the cadence of nature.

Local Insights

Guided Sessions: Many yoga and meditation escapes on the Isles of Scilly offer guided sessions that are suitable for all levels, ensuring a nurturing experience for both beginners and experienced practitioners.

Respect Nature: As you engage in these practices, remember to treat the island's natural beauty with respect. Leave no trace and allow the tranquility to linger for others to savor.

Participating in yoga and meditation escapes on the Isles of Scilly isn't just about stretching your limbs or calming your mind; it's about elevating your spirit to a place where the boundary between self and nature becomes blurred. As you breathe in the salty air and feel the sand beneath your feet, you're not just practicing yoga or meditation; you're embracing the timeless connection between yourself and the universe.

Rejuvenating by the Sea

Ahoy, fellow seekers of renewal and vitality, as we set sail on a journey that immerses us in the healing embrace of the Isles of Scilly—a realm where the rhythm of the tides becomes a melody of restoration. Our archipelago isn't just a visual paradise; it's a haven for those who seek to recharge their spirits by the sea's side. Join me as we explore the art of rejuvenation by the sea, where the salt-kissed air and gentle waves conspire to replenish your energy.

Nature's Healing Symphony

Close your eyes and envision the sea breeze carrying with it a sense of release as it brushes against your skin. Picture the sun painting the horizon with hues of gold and orange, creating a canvas of serenity. The shores of the Isles of Scilly invite you to embrace the rejuvenating power of the sea, where every inhalation carries renewal and every exhalation carries away stress.

Seaside Wellness Rituals

Rejuvenating by the sea isn't just a concept; it's a way of life on the Isles of Scilly. Begin your day with a sunrise stroll along the shore, allowing the gentle lapping of the waves to create a calming rhythm. Engage in meditation, letting the sea's timeless wisdom guide your thoughts to a place of stillness.

Thalassotherapy Unveiled

The sea's minerals and elements are your companions in this journey of rejuvenation. Wade into the shallows, allowing the saltwater to caress your skin and stimulate circulation. Embrace the ancient practice of thalassotherapy, letting the sea's bounty nourish your body.

Mindful Beachcombing
The shores of the Isles of Scilly offer treasures beyond the ordinary. Engage in mindful beachcombing, letting your fingers trace the edges of seashells and your eyes seek out intricate rock formations. In this simple act, you'll find a connection to the present moment and the wonders of the natural world.

Local Insights
Morning Rituals: Embrace the serenity of the early morning hours for your seaside rejuvenation. The soft glow of sunrise and the tranquil ambiance create the perfect setting.

Unplug and Unwind: Leave behind the distractions of technology during your seaside rejuvenation. Allow the sea's embrace to be your sole focus, inviting you to disconnect and truly unwind.

Partaking in the art of rejuvenating by the sea on the Isles of Scilly isn't just about escaping to the coast; it's about immersing yourself in a symphony of renewal. As you walk along the shore, feel the sand between your toes, and listen to the waves' gentle chorus, you're not just experiencing nature; you're becoming a part of it, and in that connection, finding rejuvenation for your body, mind, and soul.

Local Holistic Practices

Ahoy, fellow travelers on the path of well-being, as we embark on a voyage that delves into the realm of holistic harmony on the Isles of Scilly—a realm where ancient traditions and island wisdom intertwine to nurture your body, mind, and spirit. Our archipelago isn't just a visual haven; it's a sanctuary for those seeking balance and holistic wellness. Join me as we explore the local holistic practices that the Isles of Scilly offer, inviting you to align with nature's rhythms.

Whispers of Island Wisdom

Imagine the wind's gentle whispers carrying with them the secrets of generations, echoing the island's deep connection with nature. The holistic practices woven into the fabric of the Isles of Scilly offer a holistic approach to well-being—one that honors the intricate dance of your physical, emotional, and spiritual selves.

Healing from Within

Local holistic practices encompass an array of approaches, from herbal remedies and energy healing to mindfulness and the ancient wisdom of the land. As you tread upon these shores, you'll discover that the healing touch of nature extends beyond the physical realm.

Herbal Wisdom

The islands' fertile soil yields an abundance of herbs and plants that have been used for centuries to heal and restore. Engage in herbal walks, guided by knowledgeable locals who unveil the therapeutic potential of these botanical treasures. From soothing teas to aromatic poultices, the healing power of nature is at your fingertips.

Energy Alignment

Explore the art of energy healing that's been handed down through generations. Engage in practices that balance your body's energy centers, inviting a sense of equilibrium and vitality. Whether it's through Reiki or other energy modalities, you'll find skilled practitioners who can guide you on this journey.

Mindful Connection

Embrace mindfulness practices that harmonize your inner world with the island's serene ambiance. Engage in guided meditation sessions, allowing the sounds of nature to be your backdrop as you cultivate a state of present-moment awareness.

Local Insights

Seek Guidance: Engage with local practitioners who have deep knowledge of the island's holistic traditions. Their insights and expertise will guide you on a transformative journey.

Openness and Respect: Approach these practices with an open heart and a respectful attitude. Remember that you're engaging with traditions that have been cherished for generations.

Participating in local holistic practices on the Isles of Scilly isn't just about engaging in wellness activities; it's about embracing a way of life that honors the interconnectedness of all things. As you immerse yourself in the healing touch of herbs, the energy of the land, and the wisdom of mindfulness, you're not just seeking well-being; you're becoming a part of the island's ancient story of holistic harmony.

Chapter 9: Island Hopping in the Isles of Scilly

How to Island Hop

Ahoy, fellow adventurers ready to set sail on an exploration of our enchanting archipelago, as we unveil the art of island hopping in the Isles of Scilly—a journey where each island tells its own story, and every passage is a step into a new realm of discovery. Our archipelago isn't just a collection of islands; it's a tapestry of experiences waiting to be woven together. Join me as we navigate the intricacies of island hopping, where the sea is our guide and each island is a gem to be unearthed.

The Island Hopping Dance
Island hopping isn't just a mode of transportation; it's a dance of discovery. Each island presents its unique allure, from pristine beaches to historical landmarks, and island hopping is the rhythm that carries you from one enchanting destination to the next.

Planning Your Journey

Before you embark on your island hopping adventure, take a moment to plan your route. Consider the attractions, activities, and experiences that each island offers. Decide whether you'll explore for a day or linger for a while on each island's embrace.

Transportation Options

The Isles of Scilly offer an array of transportation options for island hopping:

Inter-Island Boats: These vessels form the backbone of island hopping, connecting the major islands with regular services. The boats provide a scenic ride, allowing you to savor the beauty of the sea while moving from one island to another.

Skybus: For those seeking a bird's-eye view of the archipelago, the Skybus offers inter-island flights. Gaze down upon the turquoise waters and islands as they come into view during your brief flight.

Creating Your Itinerary

Crafting your island hopping itinerary is an art of balance and exploration. Decide which islands intrigue you the most and plan your days accordingly. Consider dedicating more time to islands with a plethora of attractions and activities and save shorter visits for smaller islands where you can bask in tranquility.

Local Insights

Check Schedules: Inter-island boat and Skybus schedules can vary, so it's advisable to check the timetable ahead of time and plan your journey accordingly.

Pack Essentials: As you venture from one island to another, make sure to pack essentials like sunscreen, water, and snacks to ensure a comfortable journey.

Island hopping in the Isles of Scilly isn't just about moving from place to place; it's about peeling back the layers of each island's story. As you navigate the crystal-clear waters, you'll discover that the beauty of island hopping isn't just in the destinations—it's in the journey itself, where the sea breeze carries whispers of adventure and the islands stand ready to unveil their secrets.

Things to do on Each Island

Ahoy, fellow adventurers seeking to uncover the riches of our breathtaking archipelago! As we delve into the heart of island hopping, let's embark on a detailed journey through the enchanting world of things to do on each island—a voyage that promises an array of experiences, each island offering a treasure trove of activities waiting to be embraced. Our archipelago isn't just a cluster of land amidst the sea; it's a realm of possibilities that beckons to the curious traveler. Join me as we explore the diverse offerings of each island, where every destination reveals its unique delights.

St. Mary's: Gateway to Discovery

St. Mary's, our gateway to the Isles of Scilly, welcomes you with a blend of history and contemporary charm. Wander through Hugh Town's quaint streets, where local shops offer artisanal crafts, clothing, and souvenirs. Visit the fascinating Isles of Scilly Museum, which unravels the archipelago's history. Embark on guided walks to explore the Garrison Walls and their historical significance.

Tresco: The Garden of Tranquility
Tresco unveils the mesmerizing Tresco Abbey Garden, a subtropical paradise that thrives in our maritime climate. Explore this vibrant oasis of rare plants and colorful blooms, taking strolls along winding paths. Visit the Valhalla Museum, a unique collection of figureheads salvaged from shipwrecks, each with its own story to tell. Relish relaxation on white-sand beaches like Pentle Bay and Appletree Bay.

St. Martin's: Unspoiled Beauty Beckons
St. Martin's is an embodiment of untouched natural beauty. Embark on coastal walks that reveal breathtaking

vistas of azure waters and rugged cliffs. Discover the unspoiled beaches of Lawrence's Bay and Par Beach, inviting you to bask in tranquility. Engage in birdwatching, as the island's varied landscapes attract an array of avian wonders.

Bryher: Nature's Masterpiece

Bryher, a paradise for nature enthusiasts, invites you to explore its wild landscapes and untouched beauty. Hike to the vantage point of Hell Bay and be rewarded with sweeping panoramic views. Indulge in beachcombing along the white-sand expanses, discovering hidden treasures brought in by the tides. Embrace the island's slow pace and its rugged charm.

St. Agnes: Westernmost Beauty

St. Agnes captivates with its rugged coastline and a sense of isolation that soothes the soul. Traverse the island's paths to reach its lighthouse, where breathtaking views unfold. Engage in birdwatching, as the island's location attracts a variety of seabirds. Wander along the shoreline, where the sea's gentle embrace meets the land's untamed beauty.

Samson: A Deserted Paradise

For those seeking a taste of untouched paradise, Samson beckons. This uninhabited island invites you to discover its archaeological wonders, a testament to human history in these remote parts. Explore the unspoiled beaches, immersing yourself in solitude and nature's simplicity.

Each island of the Isles of Scilly offers a unique tapestry of experiences. Whether you're drawn to history, natural beauty, or the simple joy of exploration, these islands hold a wealth of treasures waiting to be unearthed. As you traverse from one island to another, let the spirit of discovery guide you, allowing the islands' essence to unfold before you.

Island Hopping Tips

Ahoy, fellow wanderers, as we navigate the shimmering waters of our archipelago's island hopping adventure! As seasoned travelers of the Isles of Scilly know, every voyage comes with its share of tips and tricks to enhance your experience. So, let's set our compass on wisdom and chart a course through some island hopping tips that will ensure your journey is not only smooth but brimming with unforgettable moments. Join me as we uncover the secrets to mastering the art of island hopping.

Plan Ahead, but Stay Flexible

While planning is essential, leave room for spontaneity. Island hopping can be influenced by weather and sea conditions, so keep an open mind and be ready to adjust your itinerary. Keep track of ferry schedules, Skybus flights, and other transportation options to make informed choices.

Pack Essentials

As you traverse the archipelago's gems, ensure you have the essentials on hand. Sunscreen, hats, water bottles, snacks, and comfortable shoes are your trusty companions. Don't forget your camera or binoculars to capture the breathtaking views and spot wildlife.

Weather Wisdom

Our maritime climate can be unpredictable, so it's wise to pack layers. Even on sunny days, the breeze from the sea can have a refreshing chill. Don't forget a light rain jacket, just in case the heavens decide to sprinkle their blessings.

Embrace Island Time

One of the joys of island hopping is the chance to slow down and savor every moment. Embrace the unhurried pace of island life, and let yourself truly disconnect from the hustle and bustle.

Local Insights

Local Recommendations: Don't hesitate to ask locals for their insights on the best times to travel between islands, hidden spots, and secret trails.

Check the Tide: If you're planning to explore tide-dependent areas like tidal islands, check the tide times in advance to ensure safe passage.

Island hopping isn't just about ticking off destinations; it's about relishing the journey itself. As you sail from one island to another, let the sea breeze weave stories into your memory and the beauty of each destination etch itself into your heart.

Chapter 10: Shopping and Souvenirs

Retail Therapy on the Isles

Greetings, fellow enthusiasts of exploration and curators of cherished memories! As we embark on a journey through the shopping and souvenirs of the Isles of Scilly, let me be your guide to the delightful world of retail therapy on our captivating archipelago. From unique crafts to keepsakes that carry the essence of these islands, let's navigate the charming boutiques and artisanal havens that await. Join me as we delve into the heart of retail therapy, where every shop tells a story and every purchase is a piece of the Isles to carry with you.

Boutiques and Beyond
Our archipelago, while renowned for its natural beauty, also boasts a vibrant shopping scene that caters to a variety of tastes. Stroll along quaint streets where boutique storefronts beckon with their curated displays,

offering a wide array of treasures waiting to be discovered.

Local Crafts and Artistry

For those seeking something truly unique, our islands are a treasure trove of local crafts and artistry. Visit artisanal shops where you can find handcrafted jewelry, pottery, and textiles, each piece telling a tale of creativity inspired by the natural beauty that surrounds us.

Island-Inspired Fashion

Experience the charm of island fashion as you peruse boutiques showcasing clothing and accessories inspired by our maritime landscape. From nautical themes to ocean hues, these pieces capture the spirit of the Isles in every stitch.

Keepsakes and Souvenirs

No visit is complete without bringing home a piece of our paradise. Explore souvenir shops where you can find an array of keepsakes, from postcards that capture the sunset-kissed horizons to locally made jams and preserves that offer a taste of the Isles' flavors.

Local Insights

Support Local Artisans: Many of the items you'll find in shops are created by local artisans who pour their hearts into their craft. Purchasing their work not only brings home a piece of the Isles but supports our vibrant artistic community.

Ask for Recommendations: Shop owners are often locals themselves and can provide insights into the best places to find that perfect souvenir or gift.

Retail therapy on the Isles of Scilly isn't just about acquiring possessions; it's about taking home memories and stories that will forever be tied to these enchanting shores. As you explore the shops and choose your souvenirs, let each piece remind you of the moments you've savored and the beauty you've experienced.

Unique Souvenirs to Bring Home

Ahoy, fellow seekers of cherished memories and keepers of island stories! As we set sail through the vibrant tapestry of shopping and souvenirs in the Isles of Scilly, let's dive deep into the realm of unique treasures waiting to be discovered. From handcrafted creations to mementos that capture the essence of our archipelago, let me guide you through the realm of distinctive souvenirs that will carry the spirit of these islands wherever you go. Join me as we embark on a journey to uncover the extraordinary souvenirs that are the heart of our Isles.

Captivating Creations
Beyond the ordinary, our islands offer a collection of captivating creations, each telling a tale of craftsmanship and inspiration. These souvenirs are more than just tokens; they're embodiments of the Isles' culture and creativity.

Artisanal Jewels: Discover intricate jewelry handcrafted by local artisans, each piece a reflection of the sea's allure and the islands' charm. From seashell-inspired pendants to silver bangles reminiscent of rolling waves, these pieces are wearable memories.

Pottery and Ceramics: The pottery studios of the Isles of Scilly produce remarkable pieces inspired by our landscapes. Admire vases adorned with coastal motifs, hand-painted ceramics that capture the hues of the sea, and delicate porcelain creations.

Nautical Nostalgia: Seek out nautical-themed souvenirs that celebrate our maritime heritage. From ship-shaped bookends to model sailboats, these treasures bring the allure of the sea into your home.

Edible Memories

Taste the Isles of Scilly with unique edible souvenirs that carry the flavors of our archipelago. Handmade preserves, artisanal chocolates infused with local ingredients, and island-blend teas are perfect for savoring a piece of the Isles even after you return home.

Local Craft Fairs

If your visit coincides with the local craft fairs, you're in for an even more immersive experience. These fairs are vibrant showcases of our artisans' talents, offering a chance to interact with the creators themselves. Craft fairs are usually held during the summer months, often in community halls or open spaces. Here, you'll find stalls brimming with unique souvenirs, handcrafted treasures, and artistry that reflects the essence of the Isles.

Participation and Exploration

Participating in a craft fair can be an exciting endeavor. As a visitor, you can engage with local artisans, learn about their creative processes, and even purchase unique souvenirs directly from the creators. Craft fairs are also an opportunity to immerse yourself in the vibrant local culture, as they often feature live music, delicious food stalls, and a lively atmosphere.

Local Insights

Check Event Calendars: Before your visit, check local event calendars or ask at your accommodation for information on upcoming craft fairs.

Explore Artisan Workshops: Some artisans may offer workshops during craft fairs, allowing you to try your hand at creating your island-inspired masterpiece.

Choosing a unique souvenir isn't just about acquiring an object; it's about capturing a memory, a feeling, and a connection to the Isles of Scilly. With every carefully chosen piece, you'll carry a part of our archipelago's magic with you, reminding you of the beauty that unfolded beneath our endless skies and across our tranquil shores.

Markets and Shops to Explore

Ahoy, fellow seekers of island treasures and explorers of local charm! As we wander through the colorful world of shopping and souvenirs in the Isles of Scilly, let me be your guide to the bustling markets and quaint shops that await your discovery. From lively markets that bring the community together to charming boutique shops that house an array of unique finds, let's embark on a journey through the heart of where shopping and island culture collide. Join me as we navigate the nooks and crannies of the archipelago's markets and shops, each offering its slice of island life.

Charming Boutique Shops
Our islands boast a collection of charming boutique shops that offer a curated selection of souvenirs, gifts, and treasures that speak to the heart of the Isles. Step into these cozy havens where each item has been carefully chosen to capture the spirit of our archipelago.

The Isles' Artistry: Explore shops featuring locally crafted goods, from handwoven textiles to hand-painted ceramics. These items aren't just purchases; they're pieces of art that embody the essence of our islands.

Nautical Nook: Dive into shops that celebrate our maritime heritage with nautical-themed décor, clothing, and accessories. From sailor-striped shirts to sea-inspired home accents, you'll find a slice of oceanic charm.

Village Markets

Immerse yourself in the community spirit by visiting the lively village markets that pop up in various corners of the Isles. These markets are not just places to shop; they're gatherings that bring together locals and visitors alike to celebrate island life.

Fresh Produce and Delights: Explore stalls laden with fresh produce, local delicacies, and artisanal treats. Sample island-made cheeses, jams, and baked goods, and discover flavors that are distinctly Scillonian.

Crafted Creations: Browse through stalls offering handmade crafts, jewelry, and artworks that reflect the creativity of our islands. Engage with local artisans and learn about their processes.

Recommended Locations

Hugh Town Market: Located at the heart of St. Mary's, Hugh Town Market is a vibrant hub for local produce, crafts, and souvenirs. Open on specific days, it's a delightful place to engage with the community.

Porthcressa Craft Centre: Found in Hugh Town, this center houses a cluster of workshops and shops, featuring everything from jewelry to paintings. It's a haven for those seeking unique, locally-made creations.

Island's Edge: Situated near the quay on St. Mary's, Island's Edge is a treasure trove of nautical-themed items and maritime memorabilia. It's the perfect stop for sea enthusiasts.

Local Insights

Ask for Recommendations: Locals are your best resource for discovering the hidden gems, from quaint shops down charming alleys to pop-up markets that may not be on the tourist map.

Opening Hours: Note that some shops and markets may have specific opening hours, especially during the off-peak season.

Exploring the markets and shops of the Isles of Scilly isn't just about acquiring goods; it's a journey that allows you to connect with the pulse of our island culture. Each market stall and boutique shelf is a window into our community's creativity, and every purchase is a piece of our archipelago that you can carry with you, long after you've returned home.

Chapter 11: 7-Day Itinerary

Day 1: Arrival and Island Orientation

Ahoy, fellow adventurers, and welcome to the Isles of Scilly! As your local guide, I'm thrilled to kick off your 7-day island adventure with a day of arrival and island orientation that will set the tone for the incredible journey ahead. Let's dive into the details of your first day on our beautiful archipelago.

Morning: Arriving in Paradise

Your journey begins as you step off the Skybus or disembark from the ferry onto the enchanting St. Mary's Island. Take a moment to inhale the fresh sea breeze and let the tranquility of the Isles wash over you. Your accommodation awaits, and whether you've chosen a cozy B&B, a charming cottage, or a luxurious resort, you'll find a warm Scillonian welcome.

Afternoon: Stroll through Hugh Town

After settling in, take a leisurely stroll through Hugh Town, the heart of St. Mary's. Meander along its charming streets, where pastel-hued houses are adorned with colorful gardens. Boutiques, art galleries, and local shops beckon with unique finds and treasures waiting to be discovered.

Lunch with a View

Savor a delicious lunch at one of the town's quaint cafes or beachside eateries. From freshly caught seafood to hearty sandwiches, each bite is a taste of our island's flavors.

Evening: Sunset over Porthcressa Beach

As the day starts to wind down, head to Porthcressa Beach to witness a breathtaking sunset over the azure waters. Find a comfortable spot on the sandy shores or settle on a bench, and watch as the sun paints the sky with hues of orange and gold. It's a moment of serenity and beauty that will leave you in awe.

Orientation Tips

Pick up a Map: Before you set out, grab a map of St. Mary's from your accommodation or the tourist office. It will help you navigate the island with ease.

Ask the Locals: Don't hesitate to strike up a conversation with locals if you need directions or recommendations. We're a friendly bunch!

Day 1 is all about unwinding, absorbing the island's pace, and setting the stage for the adventure that awaits. From the charming streets of Hugh Town to the stunning sunset at Porthcressa Beach, you'll already feel the magic of the Isles seeping into your soul.

Days 2-3: Coastal Exploration and Water Adventures

Ahoy, intrepid adventurers! As the sun rises on Days 2 and 3 of your island adventure, it's time to embark on a journey that will have you exploring the captivating coastal wonders and diving into exhilarating water activities. With Tresco as your playground, prepare to be enchanted by the sub-tropical beauty above and below the waves.

Day 2: Tresco Abbey Garden and Beyond
Morning: A Sub-Tropical Paradise

Today, hop aboard an inter-island boat that will whisk you away to Tresco, where the world-renowned Tresco Abbey Garden awaits. Stroll through this enchanting oasis of exotic plants, vibrant blooms, and hidden pathways. It's a paradise that will transport you to different corners of the globe, all while staying within the embrace of the Isles.

Lunch with a View

Enjoy a delightful lunch at the Garden's café, where locally sourced ingredients and garden-fresh flavors take center stage. Savor your meal amidst the lush surroundings that make Tresco Abbey Garden a haven of serenity.

Afternoon: Underwater Discovery

For the afternoon, don your snorkeling gear or join a guided kayaking excursion to explore the crystalline waters around Tresco. The vibrant underwater world is teeming with marine life, from colorful fish to curious seals. Immerse yourself in this aquatic realm, and let the wonders beneath the surface captivate you.

Day 3: Ocean Adventures and Island Hopping
Morning: Sailing to Uninhabited Isles

Set sail on a boat excursion that will take you to uninhabited isles with pristine beaches and hidden coves.

Bask in the sun's warmth and let the rhythm of the waves soothe your soul. Feel the sand between your toes as you step onto shores untouched by urban life.

Lunch on the Beach

Indulge in a picnic lunch on one of these secluded beaches, relishing the flavors of a meal shared in the embrace of nature.

Afternoon: Snorkeling Expedition

Plunge into the crystal-clear waters for a snorkeling expedition that reveals the vibrant marine life beneath the waves. Snorkel amidst underwater gardens, spot playful seals, and feel a sense of connection with the ocean's mysteries.

Island Insights
Booking Ahead: Remember to book your boat and water activity experiences in advance to secure your spot.

Snorkeling Equipment: Some tours provide snorkeling equipment, but you can also bring your own if you prefer.

Days 2 and 3 bring you face-to-face with the astounding beauty of our coastal landscapes and the exhilarating adventures that await in our waters. From the lush realms of Tresco Abbey Garden to the underwater enchantment of snorkeling, these days will leave you with memories that shimmer like the waves under the Scillonian sun.

Days 4-5: Nature Immersion and Cultural Experiences

Ahoy, fellow wanderers! As the sun graces the Isles on Days 4 and 5 of your island adventure, it's time to delve deeper into the heart of the Scilly archipelago. St. Martin's is your canvas for the next two days, promising nature's embrace and enriching cultural experiences that will leave you captivated.

Day 4: St. Martin's Treasures

Morning: Pristine Beaches and Island Hiking

Begin your day with a leisurely stroll along St. Martin's white sand beaches. Breathe in the pure sea air and listen to the soothing lullaby of waves. Then, embark on a scenic hike to the Daymark, where panoramic vistas of the Isles and beyond await.

Lunch with a View

Savor a delicious beachside lunch, relishing in the flavors of local produce and freshly caught seafood. It's a taste of island life that nourishes both body and soul.

Afternoon: Exploring Art and Creativity

Immerse yourself in the island's artistic tapestry by visiting the studios of local artists. Engage in conversations about their craft and discover the inspirations that fuel their creativity. As you witness their works come to life, you'll gain insights into the soul of St. Martin's artistic community.

Day 5: Hidden Coves and Hidden Depths

Morning: Hidden Coves Discovery

Venture off the beaten path to uncover the hidden coves that dot St. Martin's coastline. These secluded gems are invitations for quiet contemplation, beachcombing, and moments of pure serenity.

Lunch with a View

Enjoy a picnic lunch amidst the natural beauty of your chosen cove. The gentle sound of waves and the open sky provide the perfect backdrop for a memorable meal.

Afternoon: Beneath the Waves

Join a guided snorkeling excursion to explore the underwater realms surrounding St. Martin's. Glide over rocky formations, encounter marine life in their natural habitat, and witness the mesmerizing dance of light beneath the surface.

Island Insights

Art Studio Visits: Check with your accommodation or the local tourism office for a list of open art studios and their operating hours.

Tidal Awareness: When exploring hidden coves, be aware of the tides to ensure your safety.

Days 4 and 5 bring you a fusion of natural wonders and cultural gems. From hiking to hidden heights to immersing yourself in the artistic heartbeat of the island, you'll find that St. Martin's offers a rich tapestry of experiences that celebrate both the land and its people.

Day 6: Wellness and Tranquility

Greetings, seekers of serenity and well-being! Day 6 of your island adventure is an invitation to slow down, recharge, and immerse yourself in the restorative embrace of Bryher. As your local guide, I'm excited to guide you through a day dedicated to wellness, tranquility, and the harmonious connection between body, mind, and nature.

Morning: Yoga by the Sea

Wake up to the gentle lapping of waves and the fresh island breeze. Begin your day with a sunrise yoga session by the sea. The rhythmic ebb and flow of the tides provide a natural rhythm that enhances the practice, creating a sense of oneness with the elements.

Healthy Breakfast

After your yoga session, indulge in a nourishing breakfast that fuels your body for the day ahead. Many accommodations offer locally sourced ingredients, ensuring that every bite is a taste of Scilly's bounty.

Mid-morning: Nature Walk and Beach Meditation

Embark on a leisurely nature walk, allowing your senses to absorb the island's tranquility. Pause at a pristine beach, where you'll partake in a guided meditation session. Let the soothing sound of waves and the rustle of leaves lull you into a state of deep relaxation.

Lunch: Farm-to-Table Delights

Savor a farm-to-table lunch that celebrates the Isles' agricultural bounty. Fresh vegetables, locally caught fish, and artisanal cheeses come together to create a culinary experience that nourishes both body and spirit.

Afternoon: Beachcombing and Rejuvenation

Spend your afternoon beachcombing along Bryher's shores. Collect shells, polished stones, and fragments of sea glass as mementos of your tranquil day. As you connect with the land and sea, you'll find a sense of renewal and rejuvenation.

Sunset Reflections

As the sun sets over the horizon, find a quiet spot to reflect on the day's experiences. Write in your journal, capture the moment with a sketch, or simply sit in contemplation as the colors of the sky evolve with the fading light.

Island Insights

Yoga Equipment: If you're a yoga enthusiast, consider bringing your own mat to enhance your practice.

Disconnect to Reconnect: Embrace the opportunity to disconnect from digital devices and fully immerse yourself in the island's tranquil beauty.

Day 6 is an oasis of well-being and tranquility amidst the vibrant adventures of your week. From yoga by the sea to beach meditation and moments of reflection, you'll find that Bryher's serene landscapes provide the perfect canvas for nurturing your inner harmony.

Day 7: Farewell and Reflections

Greetings, intrepid explorers, as you embark on the final day of your unforgettable island odyssey. Day 7 is a day of farewells and reflections, a time to savor the memories you've made, and to carry the spirit of the Isles with you as you depart. As your local guide, I'm here to help you bid adieu to the Scilly archipelago with a sense of fulfillment and gratitude.

Morning: A Last Glimpse of Paradise

Wake up early to catch a final glimpse of the Isles bathed in the soft light of the morning sun. As you step outside, take a moment to absorb the tranquility and beauty that have been your companions throughout the journey.

Breakfast and Packing

Enjoy a leisurely breakfast, savoring each bite as you reminisce about the adventures of the past week. Take your time packing your belongings, ensuring that you've gathered all the treasures and memories you've collected.

Mid-morning: Stroll and Souvenirs

Take a leisurely stroll through Hugh Town, allowing yourself to immerse in the familiar sights and sounds that have become dear to you. Visit local shops and boutiques to pick up souvenirs and gifts, each one a tangible reminder of your time on the Isles.

Lunch: A Scenic Farewell

Indulge in a scenic lunch, perhaps on a beachside terrace or overlooking the harbor. As you savor each bite, let your thoughts drift to the experiences you've had, the landscapes you've explored, and the friendships you've formed.

Afternoon: Reflection and Farewell

Spend your afternoon in quiet reflection. Find a peaceful spot, whether it's on the shore or in a serene garden, and take the time to jot down your thoughts and impressions of the week. Consider the moments that moved you, the beauty that touched your soul, and the connections you've made.

Sunset Farewell

As the sun begins its descent, find a vantage point to witness the sunset one last time. Let the colors of the sky inspire a sense of gratitude for the journey you've undertaken and the memories you'll carry with you.

Island Wisdom
Capture the Moments: Keep your camera or journal close to capture the final glimpses of the Isles and the emotions they evoke.

Exchange Contacts: Exchange contact information with fellow travelers and locals you've connected with. It's a way to keep the spirit of the Isles alive.

Day 7 is a bittersweet farewell to the Isles of Scilly. As you reflect on the experiences that have enriched your soul, remember that the beauty, serenity, and magic of these islands will always be a part of you. Carry these memories forward and let them inspire your future adventures.

Chapter 12: Practical Information

Health and Safety Tips

Hello, fellow travelers, and welcome to the section that puts your well-being first. As you venture through the enchanting Isles of Scilly, it's important to prioritize your health and safety. Here, I'm to provide you with some essential tips to ensure that your journey is as safe and enjoyable as possible.

1. Sun Protection
The Isles are blessed with ample sunshine, which means protecting your skin from the sun's rays is crucial. Pack sunscreen with a high SPF, sunglasses, a wide-brimmed hat, and lightweight, long-sleeved clothing to shield yourself from UV exposure.

2. Tidal Awareness
Many of our island landscapes are influenced by tides. It's important to be aware of tidal timings, especially if you're exploring hidden coves or rocky shores. Keep an

eye on tide schedules and plan your activities accordingly to avoid getting stranded.

3. Footwear for Exploration

As you explore our coastal paths and beaches, comfortable and sturdy footwear is a must. Choose footwear that offers good grip and support, as some trails can be uneven. Sandals may be suitable for the beach, but sturdy shoes are recommended for hikes.

4. Stay Hydrated

It's easy to forget to stay hydrated because of the excitement. Keep a reusable water bottle with you and make sure to drink enough water throughout the day, especially if you're engaging in outdoor activities.

5. Emergency Contacts

Familiarize yourself with local emergency numbers, healthcare facilities, and the location of the nearest pharmacy. In case of any medical concerns or emergencies, you'll be well-prepared to seek assistance promptly.

6. Mind the Wildlife

While interacting with the island's wildlife is a delight, it's essential to do so respectfully and responsibly. Maintain a safe distance from animals, avoid feeding them, and follow any guidelines provided by tour guides or signage.

7. Respect for Nature

Preserving the natural beauty of the Isles is a shared responsibility. Stay on designated paths, respect wildlife habitats, and avoid leaving any traces of your visit behind. Dispose of waste properly and contribute to the sustainability of the environment.

8. Water Safety

If you're engaging in water activities, ensure you're a confident swimmer and follow safety instructions from guides. Always wear provided safety equipment, such as life jackets, during water sports and excursions.

9. Weather Preparedness

Our weather can be changeable, so it's a good idea to pack layers. Even on sunny days, a light jacket or sweater can be handy, especially if you're planning to be outdoors for an extended period.

As you embark on your island adventure, remember that your safety is our priority. By following these tips and exercising care and consideration, you'll be able to fully enjoy the magic of the Isles while keeping yourself and others safe.

Useful Phrases and Local Language

Hello, fellow explorers! As you journey through the Isles of Scilly, connecting with the local community can enhance your experience and create meaningful memories. While English is the primary language spoken here, a few phrases in the local dialect can go a long way in fostering connections and showing respect for our island culture. Here are some useful phrases to add a touch of authenticity to your adventure:

1. Greetings and Courtesies

"Good morning/afternoon/evening": A warm way to acknowledge others throughout the day. In the local dialect, you might hear "Mornin'!", "Arvo!", and "Evenin'!"

"Please" and "Thank you": Courtesies that are appreciated in any language. "Please" is often replaced by "if you'd be so kind" in the local lingo.

2. Island Terminology

"Off-Islander": A friendly term for visitors, like yourselves. Embrace it proudly as you explore our home.

"Boatman": When you're looking for a boat ride between islands, asking for the "boatman" will point you in the right direction.

3. Ordering Food and Drinks

"A pint of local brew, please": A delightful way to request the local ale at a pub.

"Fish 'n chips, if you'd be so kind": An endearing phrase for indulging in one of our beloved seafood dishes.

4. Engaging with Islanders

"What's the craic?": A polite way to find out what's happening or to strike up a conversation.

"Lovely day, isn't it?": A simple way of starting a conversation that acknowledges the beautiful surroundings.

5. Farewells

"Cheerio!": A cheerful way to say goodbye and spread positive vibes.

6. Island Insights

Language Exchange: Islanders are often delighted to hear visitors attempting the local dialect. Don't hesitate to ask for pronunciation tips or translations – it's a great way to connect.

Embrace the Lingo: Embracing a few local phrases shows respect for our culture and creates genuine interactions with locals.

Using a sprinkle of the local dialect can add a touch of charm to your conversations and interactions. While English is universally understood, incorporating a few phrases will undoubtedly earn you smiles and warm receptions from the island community.

Currency, Banking, and Local Services

Hello, fellow travelers, and welcome to the practical side of your island adventure. As you explore the enchanting Isles of Scilly, it's important to have a grasp of the currency, banking facilities, and essential services available to ensure your journey is smooth and stress-free. Here's a rundown of what you need to know:

1. Currency

The official currency in the Isles is the British Pound Sterling (£). You'll find that most establishments, from shops to restaurants, accept major credit and debit cards. However, it's always wise to have a bit of cash on hand for small purchases and places that might not accept cards.

2. Banking Services

Banks and ATMs are available in the main town of Hugh Town on St Mary's Island. It's advisable to withdraw cash from ATMs in town before venturing to other islands, where banking services might be more limited. Banks typically operate on weekdays, so plan your banking needs accordingly.

3. Local Services

Post Office: The local post office in Hugh Town offers mailing and shipping services. It's a great place to send postcards or souvenirs back home.

Pharmacies: Pharmacies can be found in Hugh Town, offering a range of over-the-counter medications and health products.

Medical Facilities: There is a local medical center on St Mary's Island, ensuring that you have access to medical care if needed during your stay.

Internet and Communication: Most accommodations, cafes, and public spaces offer Wi-Fi connectivity. Mobile network coverage is generally good across the islands.

4. Tipping Etiquette

Tipping is appreciated but not mandatory. If you've received exceptional service, rounding up the bill or leaving a small tip is a gesture of appreciation.

5. Island Insights

Local Markets: Support local artisans and businesses by purchasing handcrafted souvenirs and products at markets and shops. It's a wonderful way to bring home a piece of the Isles' charm.

Small Change: Having a bit of change in coins can be handy for public transportation, small purchases, or tips.

6. Banking Hours
Banking hours can vary, with most banks operating from around 9:30 AM to 4:30 PM on weekdays. It's a good idea to check ahead if you're planning a banking visit.

Understanding the currency, banking facilities, and essential services will empower you to navigate the practical aspects of your island experience seamlessly. Whether you're sending postcards, withdrawing cash, or staying connected, these details ensure that your focus remains on the beauty and adventure that surround you.

Staying Connected: Internet and Communication

Hello, fellow explorers, and welcome to the digital side of your island adventure. While the Isles of Scilly offer a serene escape from the hustle and bustle of everyday life, we understand that staying connected and sharing your experiences is important. Here's everything you need to know about internet access and communication during your stay:

1. Internet Access

Wi-Fi connectivity is available across the islands in most accommodations, cafes, restaurants, and public spaces. You'll have no trouble sharing your stunning island snapshots with friends and family. However, do keep in mind that due to our unique geography, the internet connection might be a bit slower compared to urban areas.

2. Mobile Network Coverage

Mobile network coverage is generally reliable throughout the islands. Major carriers provide service here, so you can stay connected while on the go. Keep in mind that some remote areas might have weaker signal strength, but that's all part of the charming island experience.

3. International Roaming

Before you set off on your journey, it's a good idea to check with your mobile carrier about international roaming plans. This will help you avoid any surprises on your phone bill and ensure you have a hassle-free connection.

4. Public Phones

Public payphones are still available in some areas, particularly in the main town of Hugh Town. They accept coins and phone cards, which you can purchase at local shops or newsagents.

5. Time to Disconnect

While staying connected is convenient, remember that the Isles of Scilly offer a chance to disconnect from the digital world and immerse yourself in the natural beauty and tranquility. Take moments to relish the sounds of the sea, the feel of the sand beneath your feet, and the company of fellow travelers.

6. Island Insights

Local Etiquette: When using your phone in public spaces, especially in quieter areas, be mindful of the peaceful atmosphere and the people around you.

Digital Detox: Consider designating specific times during your island adventure for a digital detox. This will allow you to fully embrace the island's serenity.

While staying connected is important, finding a balance between technology and serene surroundings is key. Enjoy the convenience of internet access while also savoring the moments when you're truly present in the magic of the Isles of Scilly.

Essential Contacts and Websites

Greetings, fellow adventurers! In this age of technology, having access to essential contacts and reliable websites can greatly enhance your travel experience. Whether you're seeking information, assistance, or inspiration, here's a guide to some essential contacts and websites that will prove invaluable during your time in the Isles of Scilly:

1. Isles of Scilly Tourist Information Centre:

Phone: +44 (0)1720 424031

Website: www.visitislesofscilly.com

The Tourist Information Centre is your go-to resource for up-to-date information about events, activities, accommodations, and more. Whether you're looking for the best hiking trails, local events, or practical advice, the friendly staff here are eager to assist you.

2. Transport Providers:

Skybus (Isles of Scilly Travel):

Phone: +44 (0)1720 662944

Website: www.islesofscilly-travel.co.uk

Scillonian III (Isles of Scilly Steamship Company):

Phone: +44 (0)1720 334220

For booking inter-island flights and ferry crossings, these providers offer reliable transportation options to help you seamlessly explore the archipelago.

3. Accommodation Booking Platforms:

Booking.com: www.booking.com

Airbnb: www.airbnb.com

These platforms offer a wide range of accommodations, from cozy cottages to luxury resorts. They're a convenient way to browse options, read reviews, and secure your island haven.

4. Local News and Updates:

Islands FM formerly known as Radio Scilly:

Frequency: 107.9 FM

Website: www.islandsfm.org

Stay tuned to Radio Scilly for local news, weather updates, and community happenings. It's a great way to immerse yourself in island life.

5. Emergency Services:

Police: 999 (Emergency) / 101 (Non-Emergency)

Medical Assistance: 999 (Emergency) / 01720 422628 (St. Mary's Health Centre)

In case of emergencies, these numbers will connect you to the necessary services.

6. Island Social Media:

Follow the official social media pages of the Isles of Scilly for stunning photos, event announcements, and local insights. Search for hashtags like #IslesOfScilly and #ScillyAdventure to discover hidden gems shared by fellow travelers.

7. Island Blogs and Forums:

Engage with travel blogs and online forums where island enthusiasts share their experiences, tips, and recommendations. Websites like TripAdvisor and travel blogs dedicated to the Isles offer firsthand insights from those who have journeyed here before you.

Having access to these essential contacts and websites will empower you to stay informed, connect with locals and fellow travelers, and make the most of your island adventure.

Conclusion

As your journey through this travel guide comes to an end, I want to extend my heartfelt gratitude for allowing me to be your companion on this virtual voyage to the Isles of Scilly. From the moment you embarked on this exploration, I hope you've felt the wind in your hair, the sand between your toes, and the magic that only these islands can offer.

The Isles of Scilly are not just a destination; they're an experience that transcends time and space. Whether you're a nature enthusiast, an adventure seeker, a culture aficionado, or simply someone seeking respite from the bustling world, the Isles have a piece of their heart to offer you.

In your mind's eye, envision standing atop a rocky cliff, gazing out at the endless azure expanse of the Atlantic Ocean, feeling the weight of the past mingle with the promises of the future. The whispers of history, the songs of the sea, and the laughter of locals are woven into the very fabric of these islands.

From the moment you arrive, you're not just a visitor; you're part of a story that spans generations. You're welcomed by the warm smiles of islanders who know that the true treasure of these lands is the community that thrives upon them.

As you traversed the pages of this guide, you've explored pristine beaches, wandered through lush gardens, ventured into the wilds of nature reserves, and indulged in culinary delights that pay homage to the bounty of the sea. You've navigated the ins and outs of island hopping, engaged with local artisans, and found solace in wellness retreats by the sea.

Remember the sunsets that painted the skies with hues of gold and crimson, the laughter shared with newfound friends, and the quiet moments of contemplation as you listened to the song of the waves. These memories are yours to treasure, to revisit in the pages of your heart whenever life calls for a retreat to tranquility.

As you embark on your own personal journey to the Isles of Scilly, whether physically or through the captivating narratives within these pages, remember that the islands await with open arms. They're not just a destination; they're a state of mind—a refuge for the soul, a playground for the curious, and a canvas for your stories.

So, as the tides ebb and flow, and as the sun kisses the horizon, may the spirit of the Isles of Scilly forever reside within you, reminding you that adventure, wonder, and beauty are always at your fingertips.

Thank you for allowing me to be your guide, your storyteller, and your companion. Until the day your footsteps grace these shores, may your heart find solace in the timeless allure of the Isles of Scilly.

With warm wishes for your journey ahead,

Larry E. Miller.

Printed in Great Britain
by Amazon